BE THE LEADER
YOU ARE BORN TO BE

BE THE LEADER YOU ARE BORN TO BE

FB: Brion T Connolly
betheleader.tv

Copyright©2020 by Brion T Connolly
All rights reserved. Written permission must be secured from the publisher or the author to use or reproduce any part of this book, except for brief quotations in critical reviews or articles.

ISBN: 978-0-578-67126-0

Cover design by 360 Media Group
Page layout by Win-Win Words LLC
Author photos by www.timwestphotography.com

Printed in the United States of America

CONTENTS

	Introduction	ix
1	**Self-Management**	2
	Self-Control and Integrity	3
	Temperance	4
	Power of a Positive Attitude	6
	Become an Unshakable Optimist	10
	Healthy Self-Esteem	11
	The Power of Laughter	13
2	**Benefits of Continuous Learning**	16
	Learn What Made Other Leaders Successful	18
	Benefits of Leadership Skill Training	20
	Become a Lifelong Learner	22
	Commuting University	24
3	**Lead by Example**	28
	Believe in Yourself and Your Vision/Dream	30
	Be Your Own Best Advisor	31
	Be Your Own Best Coach	34
4	**Self-Actualization**	38
	Psycho-Cybernetics	40
5	**Time Management**	44
	'Think Time'	44

	Great Leaders as Outstanding Time Managers	45
	A Daily Activity	47
6	**Vision Tools**	50
	Reinforcement from Self-Talk	50
	The Future Lens	54
	Elements of a Future Lens: Visuals, Pictures	54
	Write a 'Wikipedic Entry'	62
	Use the Power of Positive Music	63
	Reinforce Ideas Daily	65
7	**Mindsets**	68
	Have High Expectations	68
	Anticipate Obstacles	70
	Overcoming Adversity	70
	Avoid Distraction	74
	The General Upward Direction	76
	Become Solution-Oriented	76
8	**The Power of Decision**	80
	A Leader Must Be a Critical Thinker	81
	Kill Procrastination	83
	Self-Discipline: The Master Key	85
	Commitment/Stick-to-it-tiveness	87
	Sense of Humor	89
9	**Develop the Enduring Quality of Perseverance**	92
	Stay Strong	93
	Failure's Greatest Teacher	94

	This Too Shall Pass	96
	Success Breeds Success:	
	The Snowball Effect	97
	Finish Strong!	98
10	**Become a Master Communicator**	**102**
	Effectively Communicate a Clear Vision	105
11	**Managing Others**	**110**
	Leadership Is Influence	110
	Master Human Psychology	112
	Develop a System of Accountability	113
	Connectivity	114
	Understand People	115
	Personality Magnetism	117
	Keep a Healthy Distance	118
	A Steel Fist in a Velvet Glove	120
	Treat Subordinates as Individuals,	
	Not Numbers	121
	Add Value to Others	123
	Conflict Resolution	124
12	**Leadership Practices**	**130**
	Trust Brings Respect	130
	Use Productive Ideas from	
	All Levels and Reward Accordingly	130
	Attract and Develop Other Leaders	133
	Being Accountable to Everyone	135
	Empower Others	136
	Maintain Communications	138
	Insight Ability	140
	Look for Results Versus Activity	141

	Take Action	143
	Find a Way for the Team to Win	145
	Ability to Persuade: Get Buy-in from Subordinates	147
13	**Operate in a Streamlined Mode of Operation**	**152**
	Establish a Mode of Operation for Others to Admire and Copy	154
	Be Organized: Simplify	156
	Prepare in Advance	159
	Leaders Respect Authority	161
	Entrepreneurial Instinct about What Will Sell: Know Your Business	162
14	**Practical Matters**	**166**
	Diet & Exercise	166
	Protein for Strength, Carbohydrates for Energy	166
	Control Your Media Intake	167
	Crushing Addiction: Support Groups	168
	Money Management	169
	BONUS: A Belief System that Works	170
	The Author	173

INTRODUCTION

Talent as Waterford Crystal

YEARS AGO I WAS GIVEN ONE OF THOSE so-called 'psychological tests' by someone who claimed it could reveal much about one's character and identify his or her desires for the future.

In fact, a lot of it was surprisingly revealing to me.

One question on the test was about vocation and it said to ". . . think of a container and then, what would you do with it?" I chose a cut Waterford crystal wine glass, which I would hold up to the sunlight so I could watch the prismatic effect of the light rays passing through the cut glass, shooting rays of colored light!

Yeah, there's always someone like me in every crowd.

That answer, though, accurately and honestly described how I feel about work: it should be something cherished. That is, everyone should be living life to the fullest doing what they love. One of the great tragedies of human history is that, for whatever reason, most people never reach the zenith of exercising their favorite skills for monetary gain or even for the satisfaction of doing the work they love.

This is one of my deepest longings—to see everyone using their gifts and talents to their fullest degree.

I believe that everyone is born with a blueprint in their soul. If you are living in a free society where there is opportunity, then you should have the freedom and even the expectation to do all that you can to maximize your gifts and talents to the benefit of others. Your job should be something that you do to make the world a better place.

Waterford Crystal is not made by just any factory worker. A Waterford factory worker has to be trained and tested worthy to be able to advance to a position as master cutter.

Likewise, your development of your own gifts and talents takes time. The key is to get headed in the right direction early in one's schooling. If you don't identify until later in life what primary skill it is on which you want to focus, then by all means you should make the necessary effort to learn all that you can from all the experts along the way. It's never too late to start. Treat the nurturing and development of your talents as a task as precious as being the master cutter who produces the impeccably clean-cut Waterford Crystal. Work hard at your skill, and in time you will see that it will benefit mankind and be appreciated in its own right.

* * *

Leadership is a hot topic in a hot economy. Actually, leadership as a hot topic is nothing new, and it never gets old. The need for positive, talented, compassionate leadership is always in demand for every generation.

My chapter titled "Steel Fist In a Velvet Glove" (style of management) refers to the politically correct scenario that exists in a global marketplace in which the pressure to produce *fast* and ship *now* co-exists with an environment that expects conformity to a set of standards reflecting the mores of the 'politically correct' society.

It is a veritable minefield at times.

I do not claim to be a guru or have all the answers. What I can claim is having worked in a variety of fields including public seminar leadership, in-house corporate training, intense sales environments, financial services, and real

Introduction

estate training and licensing, as well as several community-based activities such as church membership and service (music and teaching).

I have raised three good children, and they are productive and connected.

My faith is the most important element in my life, which is why I don't hide my belief that the universe is controlled by a benevolent supreme being. I also recognize that there will always be things out of control of the leader in any company or organization. Those things over which a leader does have in control require proactivity and discipline of application.

Ultimately, this book debunks secular humanism as it applies to leadership in the marketplace. I propose we work in tandem with a higher power.

Because we are humans, our lives always involve a balance between what can be controlled and what can't. The good news is that good stuff happens, and whoever adheres to a focused mission, which in some way benefits the lives of others by offering products or services available at fair prices, will be rewarded. I believe that.

You are encouraged to read all the reference chapters in this book and to absorb them, meditate on them, and incorporate them into your life. Keep whichever ones you feel help you the most, and feel free to discard the ideas you believe won't work for you.

Out of all this, what I want more than anything else is for professionals to operate at their highest productive levels, while being happy doing something they love and getting fairly compensated for their outstanding work.

BE THE LEADER
YOU ARE BORN TO BE

SELF-MANAGEMENT

1. Self-Management

SELF-MANAGEMENT PRECEDES EVERYTHING ELSE. No one wants to follow a leader who doesn't practice what he preaches. People who are paid too much money or desperately need to hang onto their job for survival needs might be willing to put up with such a leader, but their hearts will not be in it. I assume no one wants a staff under them that gives a half-hearted effort.

You've probably heard of the parent who says, "Do what I say, not what I do!"

Your leadership should be exemplary, but you do not have to be perfect. What you should do constantly is strive for mastery of leadership qualities. If you make mistakes, pick yourself back up and move on—that's a big part of mastering leadership. Your staff will see the genuine effort, and they will respect you for it.

All my principles set forth here are building blocks; they build upon one another. This basic concept of self-management is tough. It takes discipline. When you veer off course, you reset your personal compass to your 'crystal clear' vision of who you are and where you're going. And you stick to that.

Self-discipline is the single-most important quality you can possess. This is why military training emphasizes it the most. In times of war and when bullets are flying and lives are at stake, there is no room for indecision or undisciplined behavior.

You do not have to have military training to be a successful leader, but it helps. (Why do you think the marketplace is quick to put a value on it? They know there will be an element of it in decision-making, regardless the setting.)

Self-Management

If your longer-term vision is crystal clear, self-management and discipline are easier to exercise and maintain. You must be able to manage yourself before you can manage others. Same goes with leadership.

Self-management integrates all the key elements of a productive life. This includes general principles of health: spiritual, emotional, mental, physical, and social, as well as financial. This means establishing a well-ordered manner of living: a routine of sleeping well; personal grooming and cleanliness; a time for reflection and personal inspiration; and a manner of dealing fairly and kindly with others. It means keeping your life's priorities in order—for me, those are faith, family, friends, fulfillment in work, and finance.

What are your life's priorities? If you wish, you can use mine. No charge.

One of my key purposes is to help those who have a specific technical or creative skill also learn how to better understand and deal with people. If you can't do the latter, the former stands a good chance of going to waste.

Self-Control and Integrity

An inability to properly manage yourself could very well eliminate your chances of becoming a great leader, despite whatever talents and skills you might have mastered. Your lack of ability to be self-managed becomes evident later in your career. There are many unforeseen factors that can expose a lack of self-control, usually related to moral, relational, or mental health issues.

As I write this, I just read in the *Wall Street Journal* (recommended reading, by the way) about a major money manager who was accused of fraud. What good is it to be successful in the world's eyes if behind the scenes you are acting dishonestly or unethical in some other manner?

What some cynics decry as "old-fashioned" values actually set the standard by which you should be living. When I hear someone criticize certain beliefs or social mores as "old-fashioned," what I hear them saying is that those things are inconvenient for them—an annoyance to be pushed aside—where the ends justify the means.

I am an advocate of dealing with integrity in the marketplace and in your personal life. Integrity is the congruency between what one believes and what one says or does. Count me among those who value proactiveness in the market to achieve the highest possible market share or increased sales. Yet, it must be accomplished with the underlying character quality of honesty.

One of the keys to staying properly self-managed is to have a small circle of close friends, preferably of the same gender (to avoid any 'soap opera' issues). These are people that you know you can share with confidentially. These are trusted confidantes who will give you objective feedback and challenge you to be your best.

Temperance

I am going to mention it here, and some people will think that it goes without saying: leaders must not allow themselves to get stuck in the trap of alcoholism or substance abuse. If the stresses of managing a business or people get to be too much for one person to handle, then maybe it's best if you vacate the board room and exercise your marketplace skill as an independent worker. History has lost a lot of talent to drug overdose or to tragedy related to excessive alcohol use.

Self-Management

Life should be lived and understood from the top down.

I believe in a benevolent higher power, or God, who created and controls the universe. In regard to the affairs of men, a strange dichotomy, or paradox, exists whereby God knows the future, although man can exercise free will when it comes to choosing evil or good—in effect determining his own destiny. There is a famous song lyric that says, "Life is what happens while you make other plans" (John Lennon). Chart a course and do your best to stay on it.

Because of my religious beliefs, I begin my day in gratitude inspired by contemporary inspirational music and prayer, for which I have a very specific list to be prayed over for myself, my wife, our children, etc.

I then do my best to exercise daily or at least every other day with mostly a stationary bike and some power walking.

During my time of daily prayer, I begin a log, or a to-do list with two columns—one for things I need to accomplish in the marketplace and the other listing those things I need to do in regard to the relationships in my life.

One of the first personal-development books I ever read (I was seventeen at the time) was *How to Get Control of Your Time and Your Life* by Alan Lakein. This is where I learned the basics of time management and prioritization. When I make my list, I use his principles and check them off during the day, giving priority to the most important tasks.

As a leader, you have to look at life as a whole instead of a large assortment of pieces. I used to separate my life into two boxes: personal and business. To some degree I still do this, but I also know to cut off business when I am focusing on personal relationships (especially my marriage). However, as I've gotten older (I am fifty-nine at this writing), I look at things more big picture.

Self-management involves *everything* about your life. You also must be a person who is *congruent*—someone whose words and actions align. Hypocrisy is something that is despised and even punished, severely in some cases. Look at the example of comedian and actor Bill Cosby, one of my childhood heroes. He had decades of great achievement in entertainment; his family sitcom was hugely popular and in syndication for many years. Then his hypocrisy was revealed in his mistreatment of women. How he lived with himself that way for so long is a mystery to me. Unfortunately, a single flaw in one's character can create a domino effect of destruction in one's life and sometimes the lives of many others. Beware and take care.

Power of a Positive Attitude (Attitude is Everything)

Zig Ziglar, one of the original great motivational speakers, was famous for his statement, "Your altitude is determined by your attitude." I have a YouTube video of just under six minutes available online entitled *How to Get Motivated and Stay Motivated*. In it, I share four key principles, the first of which is the Power of a Positive Attitude. This concept is timeless and oft repeated. There is never a good substitute. A positive attitude doesn't just happen. You have to have personal discipline and awareness in order to maintain a positive attitude most of the time.

I once worked with a person in the music business who performed double duty as a soundman and bus driver. Yet he had such a negative attitude, that after a while you could not stand being around him. The only problem was that he owned the sound system and the bus, so we had to put up with him. Ha! Thankfully, that lasted only two years.

Self-Management

The really sad part was that I am not even really sure if he was aware of it.

There are several things you can do to keep a good attitude. One is to follow the basics of good health: eat right, exercise regularly, and get a good night's sleep. Prayer, meditation, and journaling are good practices as well—dealing with and warding off stress are also essential to good health.

There's more to this health thing. Reading good, positive books is good for your peace of mind, as is keeping company with positive, motivated individuals. Above all, keep good relationships with your spouse and children as well as your co-workers and customers. These are people you see regularly—treat those relationships with care.

Peace and harmony can contribute to a good attitude, but trouble will eventually come, and the key in those unwanted situations is to maintain a good attitude throughout. Sometimes it comes down to just having a good relationship with yourself and having a good talking to in your own mind or in the mirror to get yourself back on track.

It's been written by several reputable writers to "think about your thoughts."

Have the ability to step back from yourself and look within at why you think the way you do. This skill of self-examination is indispensable.

When you sense you are dissatisfied with the way things are, you can readjust and refocus. You can examine why you feel a certain way. You can discuss it with a trustworthy friend or advisor and get a second opinion. This isn't about being your own worst critic; it's about being your best advocate, yet willing to admit and face your flaws.

One of the most effective ways for me to get a handle on my attitude is to think of all the things for which I am grateful. I go over them one by one, sometimes even speaking them aloud, from the top down. As soon as the list gets long enough, I usually scold myself for slipping into negativity and letting things get that far out of whack.

Make it a goal to develop a reputation for being a person with a good attitude.

People are drawn to it. Business thrives on it. When you have a good attitude, co-workers like you, and customers like you. A good attitude is contagious. On days when things aren't going well, or you don't feel well, fake it. Yes, fake a good attitude. Maybe you always wanted to be an actor or actress. Well, here's your big chance.

Altitude is determined by attitude, and it will open doors for you and pave the way to success. Make it a point to be proactive about maintaining a good attitude, and the process will reap rewards for you over and over.

Maintaining a positive attitude can be hard work. It involves mental discipline. The ability to get out of bed every day, regardless of circumstances at that time, is crucial. You must *decide* to do it. It can be harder for someone with a physical or psychological condition that *should* be analyzed and treated; however, most humans must learn how to do it themselves.

Building a positive daily attitude starts immediately at wakeup. This is exactly why I begin every day by listening to inspirational and uplifting music along with praying over specific things. I have a Future Lens of things I am aiming for and my Wikopedic Entry of what I hope I will be remembered for. One of the most powerful business concepts ever taught was motivational author Steven Covey's "Begin with the end in mind." Visualize yourself living the life you desire and, somehow, little by little, move yourself toward it.

Self-Management

Or, if time and finances allow, take quantum leaps.

All of this 'visioncasting' is preceded by an overriding sense of hope and determination. Decisions must be made throughout the day to conscientiously toss out negative thoughts, combat negative thinking, and order one's thinking aright.

We are living in a time of information overload, in which we are bring constantly bombarded by all kinds of media messages. Visual, audio, computers, smartphones, email, Facebook, etc. We exercise information and thought management to absorb the positive and cast off negativity.

It is important for you to seek positive input. This requires making the best use of your time, even while driving, availing yourself of what I call 'Commuting University.' While I'm driving, I choose positive material to listen to, either via a CD or plugging a device like my phone into the dashboard and listening. Airplane flights are good for this, too. The key is to control 'content intake'.

Become a lifelong learner. These days, it is not a matter of whether you are a college graduate or not (and I acknowledge that with certain professions, it still is required to have at least a four-year college degree or even more for professions in the field of medicine and law), yet in the business world itself, success depends more on what you can bring to the marketplace and make happen. Typically, a positive attitude precedes success and is often the thing that sustains a visionary or 'worker bee' through a time of adversity.

Two factors never change: 1: the ability to provide an outstanding product or service with skill, knowledge, and experience, and 2: the ability to optimize marketing opportunities, which in this day and age requires the mastery of online advertising: social media marketing.

Become an Unshakable Optimist

Optimism is a character quality that some people have naturally. That's probably because they grew up in a household in which one of their parents had that kind of mindset and passed it on to them. Others have to change themselves to become an optimist. One of the ways to become an optimist is to look at successful people and realize that it can be done.

One of the key advantages to being optimistic is that it will take you through adversity, problems, and crises. What makes one person able to barrel through adversity better than others? It is the mindset of looking at failure in terms of what can be learned from that failure, and knowing that it isn't the end of the world.

So, what makes some people more successful than others? One factor is that successful people have been willing to try new things; they failed at some and then learned from their mistakes, knowing all along that success often comes quickly after a failure.

Some people have been able to change the course of human history for millions by being optimistic and overcoming adversity. In the movie *Darkest Hour,* we see how the great British Prime Minister Winston Churchill stood up against constant pressure to negotiate with Hitler rather than press on with military preparedness.

Keep in mind how *your* optimism can affect outcomes in your own life as well as in the lives of many others. A Frank Sinatra song from the sixties tells about the ant trying to chew into and take down the rubber tree, that he had "high hopes." We have to take our inspiration where we can find it.

The characteristics of the unshakable optimist are persistence, perseverance, and never giving up. That actually was Churchill's mantra: "Never, never, never give up!"

Self-Management

Optimism is a mindset that needs to be renewed daily. It is easy to maintain if you use the written tools suggested elsewhere in this book: Written Goals, a Wikipedic Entry, a Future Lens, and Living in the Future Now documents. Utilizing those tools will keep you going and give you reference materials to study and remind yourself where you are headed.

Always remember: No one accomplishes great things in this life without plenty of trial and error, overcoming failure, and keeping a mindset of unshakable optimism.

Healthy Self-Esteem

You need a daily dose of healthy, balanced self-esteem. If you didn't get it from your parents, you can develop your own.

Healthy, balanced self-esteem is a crucial character quality for the leader. By *healthy* and *balanced*, I am referring to a realistic assessment of your strengths and weaknesses. There is a balance point between egomania and self-deprecation.

I've been acquainted with or worked for enough megalomaniacs to know they believe they can do no wrong. Avoid them like the plague. The general marketplace has plenty of leaders, supervisors, and managers who have tolerable personalities at worst.

The key to daily maintenance of self-esteem is doing something daily that will reinforce it. I do this in several ways. First of all, I start my day in prayer. I have a very specific bullet point list of people and situations I pray for. I also have a "Wikipedic Entry" that I have written as if it were the entry that people would find online regarding who I am and what I have accomplished in my lifetime. I also have a Future

Lens of people, places, and things I want to meet or see in my life, similar to what many people would call a "bucket list." Most of this is futuristic and goal-oriented. These tools keep me looking forward and motivated, and they directly affect my sense of self-esteem.

I also have a CD of myself reciting and quoting Positive Affirmations from a few scripts that are prewritten. (See the Appendix for source information of these scripts.)

This seems simple enough. Sometimes I just give myself a good talking to in the mirror to shape up, get over it, or to just forgive myself for something stupid I might have said or done.

The household in which I grew up was somewhat ambiguous. Although as a child I respected my father, he was not always affirming or positive. On the other hand, my mother was very loving and encouraging, but not smothering as some are.

Having three grown children of my own, and now grandchildren, I am keenly aware of how I believe parents should act. I was blessed to basically have a positive environment. Many are not.

I can see how growing up in a negative environment is sometimes the most difficult obstacle to overcome. It is a terrible injustice for parents to mistreat their children to the point where a negative self-esteem takes shape because of a lack of positive reinforcement. This is all the more reason why you must take personal responsibility for feeling good about yourself, and you must do it proactively.

This is why it is important to have the tools with which to basically brainwash yourself—to scrub out the negative influences from your past. Along those lines, there comes a point in your life in which you have to quit blaming your

Self-Management

past circumstances and take full responsibility for where you go from here. Like they say, today is the first day of the rest of your life. Make it good.

The sooner you realize you cannot depend on others to make you feel good about yourself, you will feel empowered. It is beautiful thing to know you can mostly control your own destiny. You can do this by honestly, and with candor, assessing your own strengths and weaknesses. Then focus on developing your strengths to overcome your weaknesses.

One of the best ways to find your strengths, outside of some type of personality assessment (which is the best way to identify your strengths), is to ask your closest friends in confidence. You might be surprised to hear what they perceive them to be. Write them down.

Also ask them about your weaknesses. Be sure to qualify by saying you will harbor no hurt feelings for an honest assessment. Even if some of it seems cruel or negative, purpose to use the information to your advantage by getting alone and taking stock. This feedback from friends can be some of the most valuable you will ever receive.

Look at it this way: They might be saving you years of trial and error by knowing what to emphasize in your life as far as strengths and what to work on and improve by way of weaknesses.

In any case, make it your daily goal to become the best well-rounded person you can be.

The Power of Laughter

In my commentary on Personality Magnetism, I refer to how a smile can light up any environment. The same goes for laughter.

I knew a sales manager who laughed consistently, and

it was sincere. He saw the lighter side of almost everything, even in down times in terms of sales. He was obviously happy and content with his place in life.

I believe laughter comes from the soul, and it is a powerful tool for leaders to possess.

Leaders tend to be serious types, and laughter or just good, clean humor can lighten the load.

People are drawn to joy, humor, and fun. Make it available to those you lead on a regular basis, and they will make it worth your while in terms of performance and loyalty. But this is not about cutting up and goofing off. Have fun, but maintain a proper professional decorum.

Every once in a while, I will rent a comedy movie on purpose. It breaks up the seriousness of life and daily responsibility.

My father once said that comedy was the most difficult of performing arts because humanity tends to gravitate toward the dark and difficult. This is mainly because people face challenges every day, and it is just easier to stay low and sad. The ability to see things from the lighter side is a true gift, I have often been amazed at a comedian's ability to see things from this perspective.

Laughter should never be at the expense of others by demeaning someone or making fun of them.

As a leader, if you infuse your communication with some degree of levity from time to time and look for some humor in serious situations, it will relieve stress and contribute to better performance overall.

BENEFITS OF CONTINUOUS LEARNING

2. Benefits of Continuous Learning

MOST LEADERS ARE AVID READERS. THEY ARE READERS who read with purpose and strategy. They have specific types of books they like to read, and more than likely they have compiled and continually update a personal list of titles they will read. Personally, I like nonfiction books pertaining to personal development and business. I also like reading the news from the *Wall Street Journal* and business news from *Harvard Business Review* and *Fast Company*.

Brian Tracy, one of my favorite personal development trainers, says that highly successful people are constantly learning new skills from reading and courses. The idea is to never stop learning.

I have a reading basket by my living room chair with books and magazines in the order I plan on reading them. I usually have one primary book I'm reading, and then if I ever want to take a break, I look at a business magazine.

Reading in the evening is good because it fills the mind with material that the mind digests overnight.

I never read horror stories or watch horror movies. I once heard a pastor say that he would not want to read or see anything on screen that he would not want to see happening in his own life. The principle of 'Good stuff in, good stuff out' is very powerful. The key is the power of choice.

I once looked at a list of the top one hundred books sold or in circulation of all time. I very selectively picked out a very few that were of interest to me and have either read them or have them in line to read.

Continuous learning can also be facilitated by watching valuable online instructional videos on YouTube. Look for

Benefits of Continuous Learning

the most valuable instructors and topics, and take notes while you watch. You can refer to these notes, preferably within twenty-four to forty-eight hours, to foster your best retention so as to eventually use the ideas in business or your personal life.

To be successful, you should view life as a continual 'university' experience.

Audiobooks are another excellent source of learning. I use them in my 'commuting' university (my car), where I am almost always either listening to a CD to learn something new, to reinforce affirmations from Scripture, or to pick up something from a motivational or personal-development teacher.

One of the benefits of continual learning is having good, fresh information in your head—information you can use for whatever scenario you might find yourself in on a daily basis. This could be a face-to-face meeting; a lecture or talk you are giving; a sales presentation; or a phone conversation.

Brian Tracy also had a stat I thought revealing: highly successful people are educating themselves on something new approximately ten hours a week.

Biographies are significant reading for leader wannabes because they are about the lives of people who have had an impact on history at some level or in some field. Many times you discover they endured a lot more adversity than you realized. In most cases, you find out there is no such thing as an overnight success. Sometimes that overnight success only came about fifteen years or so after whoever it was got started.

Learning new information can make you a leader in your business or industry. It can also take you to new industry designations or certifications. Imagine your brain is a sponge ready to soak up all the useful information you can find that is of interest to you. Do that, and you will be on your way to ever higher levels of expertise and accomplishment!

Learn What Made Other Leaders Successful

One of the most powerful principles in personal development I ever heard came from motivational speaker Tony Robbins when I heard him talk about "modeling." It was such a simple concept, yet so profound. The core idea is that if there is someone else successful that you know of in another field and you aspire to be like them, then you just start doing the same things that they do.

To arrive at that point might take radical change and could be quite difficult, but the core concept is the same throughout. It is simply modeling yourself after someone. If the person you are modeling is performing in a line of work that requires higher education or professional training, then taking that route is unavoidable, and you must do it.

There are no shortcuts in doing the type of work you love. Some work takes special training, but dare I say, most does not. However, it does require a type of experience necessary to do the job.

The key is to crash through and do it!

You need to ask yourself, How badly do I want it?

If you are driven and tenacious, it can be done. And it will almost certainly take time.

And read, read, read. Designate a certain time each day Sunday through Thursday for reading to improve yourself or gain new skills. I say Sunday through Thursday because weekends in America are almost sacred—they should be for spending time developing relationships and general leisure activity. Things tend to wind down come

Benefits of Continuous Learning

Sunday afternoon, when it's also time to start prepping for the next work week.

Make it a point to research the most successful people who are doing the type of work you would enjoy the most. Find out as best you can how they live their lives, how they got to where they are, and what you might need to do to put yourself in a similar position.

You might even study the lives of others who have passed on; historical figures who lived lives in which they impacted history in their field.

All this is hard work. There is no way around it.

Also, it is lonely at the top. Once you are in a position of actual leadership, you will have to get accustomed to the idea that you will have to develop the skill of making decisions on your own after getting input from many different sources. You will have to be your own best friend and most trusted advisor.

Make sure that the leaders to whom you are looking up have congruency—that they practice what they preach. And in some cases, you might have to "separate the fish from the bones."

The more you dig and learn about the lives of leaders you admire, you might also find out that there are certain characteristics of their lives you don't want to incorporate into your own. This often has to do with issues of morality, especially when it comes to sexual orientation, dubious relationships, or alcohol or substance abuse. Make up your own mind on this. Keep in mind that some of the best leadership talent has been lost or wasted in excess of pleasurable experiences. This has been a great tragedy throughout the ages.

Strangely enough, the same thing in a leader's personality that helps drive his or her particular strengths and talents can also be the source of their downfall or weakness; a personality disorder, or mental illness such as bipolarity, if not addressed or medicated, can cause horrendous mood swings or erratic behavior detrimental to the individual and those connected to their lives.

In any case, the opportunity to learn from the lives of others and incorporate the good and leave out the bad gives you a huge advantage, although it does not lessen your responsibility of making good decisions all along the way. It does give you the opportunity, however, to learn how to most expediently arrive at your goal of being the leader you most desire to be. You can then be true to the ideal that you have set for yourself.

> ## Benefits of Leadership Skill Training
>
> In the modern corporate world, the only way to get promoted is usually to manage people. For many, management comes before leadership skills were demonstrated. You might be masterful at your particular creative or technical skill, such as code writing, but if you are going to manage people, you are going to need training.
>
> If the company for which you work does not offer management and leadership training from within—and if it does, it should be credible leadership training—do what you must do in order to look for it on your own.
>
> I offer such training from my training practice headquartered in Nashville, Tennessee. I offer online training videos as well as onsite training at your business or organization. Hopefully, you can see this book as a good starting point.
>
> I also recommend other highly competent trainers, such

as John Maxwell, whose *21 Irrefutable Laws of Leadership* is one of the "master works" on the topic of leadership. Get a copy and devour it.

It amazes me how American education, even at the high school level but especially at the college level, does not include leadership training as required courses in tandem with technical or creative-skill courses.

Many workers get promoted to leadership positions despite having no idea where or how to begin. I suggest one place to start: understanding human psychology. That's one of the top skills a leader can have. I have a more in-depth discussion elsewhere when I touch on the Four Different Personality Types.

Once you are a leader, you will probably face more challenges troubleshooting people problems than you will technical or creative obstacles to the completion of work.

Those who understand human nature better than most typically rise to the top of their industry quicker than those who are first and foremost experts in a creative or technical skill. This is because the completion of work or projects depends mostly upon people working together in a smooth, well-ordered way.

Think of how valuable it is to have mostly talented and skilled workers working together to complete a project rather than a team fraught with dissension or given over to cliques working against each other. In such circumstances, you will spend more of your time trying to get 'teammates' to work together than you will on addressing the key components of a project pegged to a certain deadline.

In order to keep the team moving, you should always appoint a subleader or a 'go to' secondary on the team you are managing. They will understand more readily what you are trying to accomplish. Many times they will be able to act in your stead if you are away from the office for a short duration. Just make sure they are someone that the other team members will like and trust.

At some point in your career, you might need to make a decision when offered a promotion that will entail managing others. You will need to decide if that's what you actually want to do, versus just exercising your skill in a creative or technical capacity. Some people find that after managing others there is just too much hassle involved, so they backpedal into a supportive role. Maybe they just don't like people that much.

Whatever the case, if you are promoted to a supervisory position, you might eventually find that leadership training of high quality can be extremely beneficial to you. It will help you sleep at night without as many team issues on your mind.

Become a Lifelong Learner

Aside from actually performing the work you desire, this is the most important activity you can engage yourself in—learning. Books are a gold mine and wealth of information, highly underrated and at risk of losing significance (if not relevance) in this digital age.

Books on self-improvement and personal development should be given priority over fiction. Although novels can be entertaining and relaxing, nonfiction books about personal

Benefits of Continuous Learning

development contribute directly to the improvement of the quality of life. It is also worthwhile to read books authored by the most successful people in your chosen field, and in that regard I also highly recommend biographies. You will be inspired by the lives of others who have overcome setbacks and failure in their lives to achieve greatness. Most people who have achieved great success in politics, business, and the spiritual realm have a story well worth reading.

In this digital age, tools such as YouTube and other internet video sources make educating yourself so much more convenient and cost effective, beyond just watching a video on how to put together a newly bought crib or how to change the oil in your car. The key here is to be selective. Very selective!

You even want to have a plan in your head as to what type of information you want to learn about. Personally, I like the great motivational, leadership trainers as well as speakers who expound on personal development or inspirational topics. But those have great relevance to me. Your choices might be something or someone completely different, and that's what you should go for.

The main idea here is to emphasize *lifelong* when you seek out further educating or training yourself. That means it should be ongoing—daily, weekly, monthly, whatever.

In a year's time, you should be able to look back at where you started and where you ended up, and be amazed at how far you've come in learning new life-changing ideas and skills.

To some degree, I am not a huge advocate of getting a college education, although I have a college degree myself. I sometimes think I got my degree to please my parents' expectations. I have nothing against a college education or de-

23

gree, but there are other career-building options available now, such as technical or vocational schools or community colleges that fall below the four-year commitment and yet can open a door to a great-paying job and career.

Certain professions require higher level educational certification and training, no question. Doctors, lawyers, and some types of engineers fall into the category of professions that require not only a bachelor's degree but usually some sort of advanced degree as well, such as a master's or a doctorate. However, this is not always the case in the business world. To be successful, one can educate himself or herself with books and courses, and by modeling the behavior and good habits of successful people. There is one catch—you must then apply what you learn, and act on it.

One of my favorite motivational speakers is Larry Winget. I once saw him demonstrate a principle by asking his audience of businesspeople if they were "ready, willing, and able" to be more successful. He concluded that many people were ready and able, but most were not willing to do the work required to be highly successful.

Winget added that action was most important to implementing the activities that would take someone to a higher level of achievement and success.

Commuting University

You have heard me mention this a couple times already. Now it's time to avail yourself of it.

Ask yourself: Why waste valuable drive time on commercially inundated radio listening (classical stations are best) or PBS's *Marketplace*, airing at 6 P.M. Central Time, Monday through Friday. Control what you listen to!

After listening to your positive self-talk, avail yourself

Benefits of Continuous Learning

of great audio book classics such as The New King James Version of the Holy Bible as well as great motivational and success teachers such as John Maxwell, Tony Robbins, Brian Tracy, Jim Rohn, Andy Andrews, and others. You can listen to any number of great self-help and inspirational works. Be proactive about it. Do it daily.

The great thing about listening to positive text read out loud is that driving is often an activity where your mind processes something else while you are driving and the information can sink deep into the recesses of your mind. *I am not talking about distracted driving, such as while texting or doing something else that takes your mind off the road and might cause an accident.*

As I write this, I am currently listening to *The Art of War* by Sun Tzu.

Musically, I listen primarily to inspirational Christian praise & worship music by the Hillsong Young & Free Group, as well as some smooth jazz and classical music and Classic Rock and some Country.

LEAD BY EXAMPLE

3. Lead by Example

THIS IS A KEY PRINCIPLE IN LEADERSHIP. As a leader you will be under the microscope, and people will be watching. Your life will be on public display, at least to some extent, for as long as you are working in the marketplace, and especially if you are in government or clergy.

People talk about respecting leaders who actually "practice what they preach." You might have also heard the statement, "Your actions are screaming so loud, I can't hear a word you are saying." Keep this in mind especially when you are managing a tight-knit leadership team.

Honesty is still the best policy. Whether you are an honest person or a dishonest one, your peers and subordinates will figure it out soon enough.

While I'm thinking about it, here are a couple of adages to toss in here relative to what we're talking about:

- If and when you advocate something dishonest or otherwise unethical on a deal or strategy, rest assured, your team will do the same behind your back.
- If the pressure to perform by the rules is too great for you, dismiss yourself from a management position.

This matter of congruity, or 'integrity,' (an often misused buzzword) will run alongside you the entire time you are in charge.

Great spiritual leaders are known for this character quality. Regardless of your opinion of Christ, you must admit He had more impact on human history than anyone who ever lived.

Lead by Example

How do you successfully lead by example? You must know who you are and what you believe in or value the most, and you must be true to yourself. You need to do all this even if it costs you relationships or financial difficulty. If doing the right thing is going to cost you your health, that's a clue you need to get out of that position and go find something else. Doing the right thing should never be a hazard to your health, whether physical or mental.

The odd thing about being human is that life is *not* fair, but you can sleep better at night knowing you did the best you knew how and that you did it a manner that played right by the right rules. It's amazing how the universe has a way of rewarding congruity in honest thought and action.

A couple more adages to carry with you:

- If you persevere, things will turn around. Leading by example is an exercise in selflessness.
- The higher up the food chain you go, the greater responsibility you have to exercise your talent and ingenuity for the benefit of all others.

The Office of President of the United States is the toughest job on the planet.

Despite all the bashing he will receive from the press, if they, by majority, do not like him and opposing political parties attack him for his policies, he will still garner their respect if he is congruous in thought and action and generally expresses an interest in doing the right thing for the benefit of all the people.

Look in the mirror every day and ask yourself if you are practicing what you preach.

It has long been thought that Gandhi once said, "Be the change you wish to see," although his being the source of that exact quote has come into question. Regardless of the source or the authenticity, it's powerful! Character is what is revealed in you when no one is looking.

Step out into the day determined to lead by example. It might take awhile, but soon you will attract other leaders who will work alongside you to bring about improvement in the marketplace.

Believe in Yourself and Your Vision/Dream

Many children's stories carry the theme that we must believe in ourselves. Believing in yourself, however, is more difficult for those with a negative upbringing. It will take enormous inner strength to make up for this. I am referring to those who had nonsupportive or even verbally abusive parents. I told you earlier about my parents in this regard, and while I was not raised in an abusive household, I had to develop an ability to discern for myself that it was up to me to believe in myself—no one was going to do it for me. It was not until I was approaching adulthood that I got it into my head that I had talents and abilities that were valuable to others and the marketplace in general.

Through a process of philosophical searching and spiritual awareness, I eventually had a discussion with a bornagain Christian that inspired me at age seventeen to follow that belief system's path. That took a huge burden off my shoulders. I was now tapped into the source of a higher power, where I could learn how life and the world worked. However, it still was not the be-all, end-all for changing the 'scripts' in my head in terms of grasping my own self-worth.

In my early twenties, I was fortunate to come across a spiritual leader who had constructed thirty minutes' worth of the recitation of positive affirmations. All were scripturally based, giving them credibility in my mind. The recommendation by the author was to record ourselves reciting them. When we would play them back and listen, hearing ourselves declare them would make more of an impression than hearing someone else speak them. Apparently, our subconscious is impacted more by hearing our own voice than that of someone else. We are essentially brainwashing ourselves with positivity. It is similar to computer programming. We are programming our minds with positive data. I have been listening to these affirmations for thirty years. I am sure it has made a huge difference in my life overall.

As I mentioned earlier, I believe there is a God who puts a blueprint in your heart and mind, directing you on what you were born to do in this life. However, in these United States, we respect freedom of religion. This is not meant to influence you in any direction. The fact is, religious or not, you probably have a good idea down deep what it is you want to do with your life. Start writing it down! I cannot emphasize this enough. Moving yourself toward the fulfillment of your deepest desire to do a certain thing or move into a certain vocation will ultimately lead to the greatest sense of accomplishment you can experience.

Be Your Own Best Advisor

This is especially pertinent to your most important decisions. Sooner or later, you will discover that in order to be an outstanding leader, you will need to be entirely responsible for all the decisions you make.

The more you grow in responsibility, the more people your decisions will affect. It is also important to realize that you might not have the luxury of having a lot of time when making major decisions.

One of the best ways to make decisions is to use what is called "the Ben Franklin Close." It is purported that Franklin developed a very simple yet effective strategy for making decisions.

Start by drawing a line down the center of a blank piece of paper, and then write the decision you purport to make at the top of the page. On the left side of the page, write down all the negatives associated with making a certain decision. On the right side of the page, list all the positives. Include as much detail as you can. Eventually, in most cases, you will see one side of the page carry more weight than the other.

This might seem like an oversimplified way to making decisions, but it works. Try it and see next time you are in a position where you have to make a major decision.

Since you are responsible for the results of your decisions, you have to commit yourself to making such important decisions entirely on your own. You must take responsibility and be accountable for your decisions.

This is a sobering reality, but if you aspire to leadership on a larger scale than most, you will have to get used to it.

In the process of making decisions, it is valuable to have a few dependable contacts who are familiar with your field or industry with which whom can consult and receive counsel. Such reliable contacts are ones that you should be nurturing as you progress down your career path—at the point of getting offered a significant position of leadership is no time to start making those contacts. You need to be networking early in your career and keep it up over the years. Still, whether you have such reliable contacts or not, you will have to make a decision the best you can with all the pertinent information you can gather about the decision.

Lead by Example

You must never develop the mindset of being a leader who makes decisions based on what the majority of the crowd will dictate. The majority isn't necessarily right. If you do this, you will inevitably find yourself coming up against a situation where the crowd was wrong and you will be held responsible for the outcome. The crowd, being as fickle as it can be, will point the finger at you.

Let me say it again: Leadership mastery often involves making tough decisions.

I once heard that leaders make decisions quickly and change their minds slowly.

Losers take forever to make decisions and change their minds quickly.

Develop the first angle. Train yourself to sharpen your decision-making ability.

When it comes to tough decisions, the toughest are those in which lives are at stake. Take the scenario where President Harry Truman had to decide in 1945 whether to drop the first atomic bomb on Japan. Massive death and destruction would ensue; however, he knew that if he didn't do it, another one million American servicemen's lives would be lost to win the war in Asia.

That is an extreme example, but what if you had to decide to fire an underperforming salesperson who you knew had a wife and four children to support in lieu of hiring a younger salesperson with a stellar track record of production the past two years? If your bottom line was suffering some, you would have to do what needed to be done.

I have often heard the expression "tough love." Sometimes it applies, but sometimes it is an excuse. For example, maybe telling the underperforming older salesperson he needed to show immediate improvement (or else) would motivate him to improve or find work for which they would be better suited.

Maybe you are an independent contractor who desires better, faster work tools such as a more expensive laptop, or a better tablet or phone, but money is tight and the technology you have now is still functional and productive, albeit a little slower. So you wait until you have more 'capital,' a wise decision versus adding more debt.

Again, these are the sorts of circumstances that beg the Ben Franklin Close referred to earlier.

You are not always going to get it right. One of the keys, however, is when you don't know what to do, do something. Life has a way of getting you back on course *if* you have a clear, specific goal/target in mind.

Let's talk about counsel. Half of the people will say go for it; the other half will say to be cautious or don't do it. Take whatever you are told with a grain of salt. Consider the source, and if a majority emerges, that's probably the best way to go.

Also, if you have a good marriage, one where you are generally compatible and get along *most* of the time, a spouse can be an excellent source of wisdom. In my opinion, this is a result of the 'divine' order of things. If you believe in a higher power or God, and if you believe that you have been paired up with your 'soulmate,' you can usually trust the source and the feedback on major decisions. In general as a leader, you should strive to have a good marriage.

It is hard work, and just like raising good kids, it is worth it.

Be Your Own Best Coach

Occasionally you will want to reach out for help, but there is no substitute for being your own best coach. You are ac-

Lead by Example

countable for your own growth. This means having your own system of accountability.

It means having your own goals written down, and it means keeping track of your own progress. It means being able to get up every morning, look yourself straight in the eye, and be honest with yourself as to whether or not you are making the progress that you promised yourself you would do.

I find one of my best qualities is my constant awareness of how finite life is. Maybe it comes from growing older; however, reminding myself that I only have so much more time left to live motivates me to stick to my goals and do my best to crush them with action.

If I get off track, I give myself a good talking to in my head and re-align. Yes, I actually do this.

I sometimes think my goals might be too gargantuan. However, in the grand scheme of things, I once heard that it is better to shoot for the moon and hit the eagle than to shoot for the eagle and hit a rock. Goals must be achievable. Mentally, you should break them down into smaller, measurable tasks.

If you get too far off track, scare the heck out of yourself and think of what it's going to be like on your deathbed of regret. Unfortunately, most people die this way. Thinking of "should have, would have, could have," are my six least favorite words. Tag, you are it. You should not take this lightly, floating by on the lifeboat of life, aimless while time is a-wastin'.

Maybe you are not keeping your written goals in front of you enough. Pull them out and dust them off or revise them. Whatever you do, stay proactive.

How many of us have had bosses or employers who

promised us the moon and then did not deliver? We cannot depend on them to keep their word when they are mostly working for their own interests, too. Just keep that in mind. Speaking of which, I prefer to underpromise and overdeliver, with every expectation and effort to do the latter. Life is better that way.

Make a decision to be wholly self-reliant and to carry on, with your plan in the forefront of your mind, always.

SELF-ACTUALIZATION

4. Self-Actualization

OUTSIDE OF WHAT I CONSIDER TO BE THE most important information and activity that I spend time on—and I'm talking about faith-related things and the Scripture for me—concepts related to self-actualization are the most interesting to me.

Since I believe that all human beings are built from the inside out with a blueprint in their mind and soul for greatness and great accomplishments, I spend a lot of time thinking about these things for myself and for those people in my life.

One of my favorite teachings is Brian Tracy's *7 Mental Laws of Success*, one of which is the Law of Expectation. For example, if you have faith or the expectation that something can be done or come to pass, the chances of that happening are increased. This is a big part of what prayer is all about.

The key is the underlying motive. Is it for the good of all? Will it benefit mankind, or specific persons, or you in particular?

A favorite spiritual teacher of mine was the now-deceased Myles Munroe, once known as "the Pastor of the Bahamas." He had a saying that he wanted to "die empty," meaning that all his gifts and talents would be used up by the time he was dead. His fuel tank would be empty at the time of his death.

I pray this prayer for myself as well as for my wife and children.

See yourself in your future living the way you want: doing what you love (working hard *and* smart), living where you want, vacationing where you want, and all the while

Self-Actualization

prospering financially to benefit others.

The worst thing I ever hear is someone lamenting on their deathbed that they wish they'd have lived differently. Stop the procrastination! Take responsibility for where you are in life. Forget the past! What can you do with today and the future? There are things that you can do now to make your optimal life happen, even if slowly but surely—with *surely* being the important word here.

Earlier, I referred to the 'Wikipedic' entry where you write your own description of what your life was like, what you accomplished in what areas, etc. I have mine laminated, and I read it or speak it out loud every day. I also have my 'Living in the Future Now' document, in which I describe a typical day in 'my perfect life' in laminated form. I read that every morning as well.

One of the key principles taught by both time-management expert Alan Lakein and Brian Tracy is to make a description of your perfect life as detailed as possible. It gives you substance for your mind to work on—something to hang onto and work on as you work to bring it to pass.

Self-actualization applies to everything, from weight loss, to peace of mind, to good health, to vocational, and financial fulfillment, to success in relationships.

Here, again, a written 'inventory' is best. Next to your being healthy and loving , a plan for self-actualization and the fulfillment of it in your lifetime is the most important activity in which you can involve yourself.

Not only should you do this for yourself, but you should also join me in telling everyone you know of the importance of self-actualization. Spread the word. If anything, do it for your kids, because leaving them a legacy of success and financial blessing is the greatest gift you can bestow on them.

So, too, is the memory of having lived a life of going for a dream and making it to inspire them in their own journey.

Psycho-Cybernetics

In his work *Psycho-Cybernetics*, Maxwell Maltz discusses how, in the context of whatever it is you think about yourself or see yourself doing in the future, your brain is like a heat-seeking missile and will think of ways to direct you to that target. The book *The Secret Law of Attraction*, by Katherine Hurst, offers a similar principle: If you keep moving toward a very specific goal, the universe will cooperate and move you in the direction of helping you manifest that destiny.

Your mind has the amazing ability to move toward the target that you set for it.

In the Christian belief system, faith is when you believe something can happen in your or another person's life to a positive outcome. And of course, in Christianity, it has to be in line with God's will, meaning it is something that the Lord approves of for your, or another's, benefit.

A better way to think about all this is that there is power attached to the human imagination. Imagination is neutral in the sense that it will follow the law of GIGO (garbage in, garbage out). Put it another way: What you program into your mind and heart eventually comes out, good or bad.

Today's business leader has to stay aware of the development of products and services, what it takes to grow his company, how to manage the money, and how to keep his people focused. If he manages to do all that, their mind will need to be constantly moving in a positive direction.

This is why I recommend having written goals, Future Lenses, and spoken positive affirmations to listen to. They are the target boards that will inspire and motivate your

Self-Actualization

imagination to keep you moving toward a positive end. They will also stir the imagination to solve problems when necessary, which can encompass every day in the life of a leader.

There is a proverbial statement I like: "If you aim at nothing, you are bound to hit it." Know what I mean? You'd better.

Many people, I'm sorry to say, float aimlessly through life. They have no concrete plan for achieving their dreams or goals. Those are the ones who end up on that deathbed of regret I mentioned earlier.

Going back to Maltz, he goes so far as to suggest "imagination exercises," where you lie down for thirty minutes and imagine yourself being the person you want to be , and addressing that with as much specificity as you can muster.

One of the ideas he puts forth is that, most of the time, your mind cannot distinguish between reality and imagination, so it begins to program itself to have you becoming what you imagine yourself to be. Sounds neat, huh? The truth of this is proven over time. Tony Robbins suggests that we model ourselves after those we'd like to become like. We start doing the things that they do; eventually, with enough time and practice, the change becomes consistent reality.

The key here is to accept these truths to be reality and that they can influence perceptions of ourselves and others. Ultimately, we can improve our lives to the best of our ability by choice. The power of choice is the most significant tool we possess as humans.

TIME MANAGEMENT

5. Time Management

'Think Time'

PERIODICALLY, YOU WILL WANT TO DEVOTE OTHER SPECIFIC and 'improvised' times to *thinking*, referred to by one of my associates as 'Think Time.' These moments might even come to you unexpectedly or as a 'gift' of time.

Get space/time to think, pray, journal; meditate on very specific written goals. This will be the most important part of your day. Make it first thing in the morning (assuming that's when you usually get up). It will set the tone for everything else you do all day.

Vacations in the mountains or at lakeside or seaside are excellent for this. Take at least a week off in summer and another week off preferably between Christmas and New Year's to devote to thinking, reading, and writing.

Don't neglect this element (time management) of living a history-impacting life. It will make all the difference in the world.

One of the points that Amy Morin makes in her book *13 Things that Mentally Strong People Don't/Do* is that Mentally Strong People aren't afraid of spending time alone. It is not perceived as loneliness but as a time to enjoy life, to take advantage of cultural events or attractions alone, yet, more significantly, as time to think or meditate. For some this would be seen as time for spiritual refreshment or prayer or sacred Scripture study. In her chapter on this topic, Morin recommends journaling.

Think Time can also involve turning off electronics (*e.g.* television, radio, smartphone, or computer).

Think Time can be done anywhere, but it can be more productive when done in a restful, relaxing environment such as a mountaintop, beach, or public park.

Creating for yourself an opportunity to get away from the 'must-do' work responsibilities or other tasks can clear the mind and help you contemplate the bigger picture of things. Such think time can be crucial to facilitating better decisions, especially when faced with relationship challenges or when vocational and career-direction crossroads are approaching.

Successful people throughout the ages, including those who have made significant contributions to the advancement of human culture, have said that times of reflection are where epiphanies took place. They changed course or switched their thinking while producing great works of art, science, or technology.

The human brain often does its best work when the body is at rest. My father was a successful technical journalist, and another of his great ideas was to put paper and pen near his nightstand to write down any brainstorms that might hit him during the night and which he would want to follow up on the next day.

Great Leaders as Outstanding Time Managers

Essentially, if you want to be a great leader, or even a competent one, you must be a person of vision. This means having a view of your life long-term.

Think big. Why not? Plenty of empires and entrepreneurial dreams have been born out of big-picture thinking. The key is to be specific.

The best work I ever saw on the topic of big-picture thinking is Alan Lakein's *How to Get Control of Your Time and Your Life.*

One of the most valuable exercises Lakein mentions is the 'two-minute drill.' Get your hands on a stopwatch—a regular watch that includes a stopwatch function is fine—and prepare to write as quickly as possible a list to correspond to each of the following:

1. Write down everything you want to accomplish in your lifetime.
2. What do you want to accomplish in the next five years?
3. If a doctor told you today you have six months to live, what would you spend your remaining time doing?

The last exercise forces you to cut to the core of what you really value as most important in life, or what Lakein calls your ultimate "mission."

The key is to write as fast as you can because it forces you to go to the core of your psyche and pull out what you value most.

Next is a prioritization exercise. In each of the lists, you must choose the A-1 item, A-2, A-3, and on to the B's & C's in the same numerical ordering.

Voila! You basically have a life plan! This is stupendous and phenomenal! You have probably been walking around with these ideas in your head without them being in written form. Now they are, or at least they soon will be, right?

One of the profound statements made by Lakein is that if you spend 80 percent of your effort on the A's, then the B's & C's will take care of themselves.

Larger goals should be accompanied by mid-range and shorter-term goals. The idea is to make the shorter-term goals realistic and attainable.

Time Management

Once you have a fairly comprehensive list of goals, you will want to think of activities that you will need in order for you to accomplish the goals. Giving these activities priority throughout your daily routine will move you forward.

The idea of breaking down tasks into smaller 'bite-sized' pieces keeps you from getting frustrated when the BHG 'big hairy goals' seem impossible to reach.

All these goals need to be written down and prioritized. Go after your goals with a sense of urgency. The more organized you are in terms of ordering them in terms of priority, the more likely you are to spend time on the most-important activities versus the lesser.

Your goals and activities that support them should be referred to often. Use them in tandem with my Wikipedic Entry tool, and they will help you stay on track.

A Daily Activity

Managing time is a daily activity and becomes part of your mindset and DNA. The older you get, the more conscious you should become of time management.

I find that keeping my larger goals in front of me, especially with my Wikipedic Entry nearby, incentivizes me to constantly think of whether or not what I'm doing at the time is moving me toward my goals.

Again, get space/time to think, pray, and journal. Then meditate on very specific written goals; this will be the most important part of your day, presumably the first part of your day. It will set the tone for everything else you do that day.

This is where I employ and use my five most important components for this time: Prayer List; Future Lens; Wikipedic Entry; Think & Grow Rich Worksheet; and Positive Affirmations listened to in Commuting University. I must add a Daily Log at this point. It is my Master Time Management Tool.

I split the Master Time Management Tool down the middle to look like a stenographer's notebook. On the left side at the top, I place a dollar sign and then the acronym for my 'C' corporation—BCI, for Brion Connolly, Inc. Then I put in three or four priority activities for the day. For example, my activities today were comprised of writing ten pages of this book, looking at the progress of booking speaking engagements, checking on my family's real estate portfolio building business, and checking on the status of my investments. However, I do try to stay focused on reinforcement of my long-term vision with the other four elements, too. In other words, I am multitasking; taking time to think, meditate, and time plan as well.

I do not take or check texts or email, or take calls during this time; however, I do check news on online.wsj.com to see if any bombs were dropped overnight or if there was some other world situation that requires prayer. It is crucial to get in a quiet place, undistracted, undisturbed by even spouse or children, co-workers, subordinates, etc. in doing this.

Make sure you read in detail and sometimes recite your Wikipedic Entry. I literally stare at my Future Lens and glance at it periodically as I am multitasking. It is planting images of my future in my head.

The Think & Grow worksheet reminds me of my financial goals.

The reinforcement that these materials provide influence and affect everything I do all day. I typically arise between 6 A.M. and 7 A.M. central time every day and devote at least a half-hour to an hour for this time of meditation and planning.

VISION TOOLS

6. Vision Tools

Reinforcement from Self-Talk

Dictionary.com defines self-talk as "... the act or practice of talking to oneself, either aloud or silently and mentally." There is great value in this.

One of the ways to make the best use of this tactic is to record yourself reciting positive affirmations from some type of script or prewritten text. You should listen to healthy 'self-talk' or positive affirmations daily.

Earlier, in Chapter 1, I introduced the concept of speaking affirmations into your own life on a daily basis, even recording yourself and playing it back so you can hear these affirmations in your own voice. One of the best when it comes to affirmations and positive living was one of my heroes, Zig Ziglar, whom I had a chance to meet and talk with. One of the things I remember him talking about during a presentation was his two-step "Daily Affirmations" process, a summary of which follows:

DAILY AFFIRMATION

Step No. 1:

Ziglar: "For thirty days, first thing in the morning, last thing at night, by yourself, in front of a mirror, stand up straight, square your shoulders, look yourself in the eye and quietly, firmly say in the first-person present tense . . ." after which he lists a number of affirming statements such as:

- "I, _____, am a person of integrity, with a good attitude and specific goals."

Vision Tools

- "I have a high energy level, am enthusiastic, and take pride in my appearance and in what I do."
- "I am bold and confident, yet humble."
- "I have a servant's heart, am ambitious and a team-player."
- "These are the qualities of the winner I was born to be, and I fully intend to develop these marvelous qualities with which I have been entrusted. Tonight I am going to sleep wonderfully well. I will dream powerful, positive dreams. I will awaken energized and refreshed, and tomorrow is going to be *magnificent!*"

Step No. 2:

"Repeat process the next morning and close by saying: 'These are the qualities of the winner I was born to be. Today is the first day of my life and it is wonderful!'"

Motivational speakers and leaders have been doing this sort of thing for years. Some of the 'originals' who also can be good sources for material such as this include Jim Rohn, Tony Robbins, and Brian Tracy.

Spiritually speaking, for Christian inspiration, I recommend going to my favorite church planter's (missionary) site, larrytomczak.com, and looking up his 'Biblical Confessions to Build Your Faith'. I have been listening to this with my own recorded voice reciting them for twenty-seven years (which I originally recorded on cassette and then transferred to CD and is now on my iPod, which I plug into my automobile dashboard and listen to).

I am also the inventor of what I call the "Wikipedic Entry," meaning on *one* page, you write what it is for which you will be remembered.

Think big with this! I did . . . and the concepts are so huge that they are strictly confidential but do-able in a lifetime.

I previously mentioned Alan Lakein's Two-Minute Drills, in which you get in touch with your deepest heart's desires of things you want to do and accomplish with your life and record them quickly in list form in *only* two minutes.

These things can help you write a very succinct, focused Encyclopedic Entry.

I am also *big* into lamination. I have laminated my own Encyclopedic Entry, and on the back I have included my Napoleon Hill's *Think and Grow Rich* Three-Step process, regarding my life's financial goals.

For the spiritually driven, I also have a Daily Prayer List for myself and family and others around the world, in bullet point form.

I start every day in prayer, Bible study, reciting my Encyclopedic Entry, and studying my Think and Grow Rich Worksheet. I also pray over properties I'd like to own and, as a speaker, cities I'd like to speak in and the key companies in the key industries for which that city is primarily known.

My three key principles for success in vocation and ultimately, finance, include Vocational Aptitude Testing (Do What You Love, the Money Will Follow), 'Visioneering,' and listening to Positive Affirmations! Start today and you will see results begin to happen!

There are other many good ones available, which I am sure you can find on the Internet; or, better yet, write them yourself and then record them onto some type of media that you can listen to on your smartphone, which can also be plugged into your vehicle's dashboard to be listened to during your Commuting University.

Vision Tools

Following are a few key thoughts reviewing and/or summarizing about speaking positive things into your mind and, ultimately, into your subconscious:

- Repeat a concept mentioned earlier, as touted by psychology and social scientists, that you are most influenced by your own voice. So, make it positive and not negative. This is an exercise for a lifetime.
- As a person of faith, I also recommend listening to the Proverbs of Solomon and the Book of Ecclesiastes.
- Listen to yourself as you recite your own writing of Your Wikipedic Entry and your Think and Grow Worksheet.
- I use pre-recorded CDs and am transitioning to media recorded onto computer and transferred to storage in my smartphone.

The power of the subconscious mind to manifest what is seen and heard is amazing. One of the hard, cold truths, however, is What Goes In, Comes Out. Your mind is neutral in the sense that it does not discern between positive and negative. So, if it is 'fed' positive self-affirming thoughts and visuals, it will do everything in its power to make those things come to pass in your life.

Make it work in your favor with self-talk.

It is best to listen to self-talk just after waking and right before sleeping. As I am drifting off to sleep, I pray that my subconscious be filled with powerful dreams of achievement and instruction from the Almighty. I pray it for not only myself but also for my wife, children, and extended family.

Be your own best friend, coach, and mentor. Fill your mind with positive self-talk. Do it every day for the rest of your life.

The Future Lens

I am also a huge advocate of visualization; you want to visualize what you want your life to look like. It needs to be viewable on hard copy or computer screen, and you should look at it first thing in the morning and last thing at night. Subsequently, the brain will work on ways to bring that vision to pass. We're going to look on it and think on it continually.

The same can be said about the benefits of 'think time.' Einstein said that it is probable that most people are using only 15 percent of their brain's total capacity.

I am convinced that Think Time gives the brain an opportunity to facilitate some of its unused parts for problem solving and processing possibly painful or difficult emotions.

With time being the best healer of getting past life's difficult experiences, increased Think Time can help you to process the emotions associated with those experiences more quickly.

Learn to value time alone and the opportunity for more Think Time. It can lead to opportunities for more creativity and better decision making. Try using some relaxing music as well to accompany you on your journey.

Elements of a Future Lens: Visuals, Pictures

I first got the idea for a Future Lens from an inspirational writer/speaker, Mike Murdock from near Dallas, Texas, who already had something similar he called a "Future Lens." You either create it in a computer screen viewable form or, as I do, on a Bienfang foam board you can purchase at an office-supply store (two feet by three feet). A Future Lens contains pictures of what your life should look like or where it is going.

Vision Tools

I divided up mine into four quadrants, cross-wise or with a large X across a landscape view or rectangle. Because I am a religious person/Christian, I reserve the top middle quadrant of my board for my worship of the Holy Trinity or images of same as well as photos of my wife, children, and other extended family. These are viewed in tandem with my specific prayers for them. I also pray for future grandchildren.

Below that top middle quadrant I place images of an unborn child because I am pro-life; persecuted Christians in other parts of the world (primarily Communist and Islamic nations); pictures of my future staff; and my seven heroes of human history aside from Christ (who is a given): Apostle Paul, King David (& Solomon), Billy Graham, Mother Teresa, Abraham Lincoln, Steve Jobs, and Bill Gates.

I admire those heroes and want to incorporate qualities of their character and ingenuity into my own life. In his book, *Think and Grow Rich,* Napoleon Hill refers to a secret council and what you might ask them when facing decisions, yet this goes a little too far. I recommend it be more like "What Would Jesus Do?" or "How might this person think about this idea or project?" In the quadrant on the left side, I include vocational and financial goal images, including real estate properties, on the right side, I have images reflecting goals and activities relating to nonprofit or voluntary activities.

I have images of myself writing and speaking to stay focused on work activity and achievement.

I have very specific locations I desire to own, reside in, or visit before I die. I have a blueprint of a custom-built home I plan on having constructed as my primary residence; a summer residence, somewhere cooler than Nashville, Tennessee; and a beach/seaside residence.

I also have images of myself participating in certain activities such as bicycling and golf to remind me to participate in healthy activity.

I have images of myself at a healthy weight.

You get the general idea...

I cut or copy and paste images primarily from the Internet and magazines.

Don't forget the basic idea of planting positive images in your head for accomplishment.

Dr. Maxwell Maltz's book, Psycho-Cybernetics, introduces his views that a person must have an accurate and positive view of themselves before setting goals; otherwise they will get stuck in a continuing pattern of limiting beliefs. His ideas focus on visualizing one's goals, and he believes that *self-image* is the cornerstone of all the changes that take place in a person. According to Maltz, if one's self-image is unhealthy or faulty, all of his or her efforts will end in failure.

A Future Lens can also be called a dream board, treasure map, or vision map. Creating a Future Lens can be a useful tool to help you conceptualize your goals and can serve as a source of motivation as you work towards achieving your dreams. Following is some guidance in this regard:

1. **Reflect upon your goals.** Most of us have some general or vague idea about what we want out of life, what our goals are, and what makes us happy. Nonetheless, when asked directly about your conception of the good life, you might struggle to come up with specifics. To make sure that you're on track, and that you won't look back on your life with regret, it's a great idea to regularly set time aside to clearly identify your goals and aspirations in as much detail as possible. Then you should devise and articulate plans with

Vision Tools

concrete steps for achieving your aims. Creating a Future Lens can be one way to help you with this important task.

2. **Think about the big questions.** Before you get started making your Future Lens, spend some time thinking about the following general questions:
   - What, in your view, defines a good life?
   - What makes a life valuable or worth living?
   - When you are on your deathbed, what will you hope to have accomplished?

3. **Break down the big questions.** To help you answer these big questions (which can be overwhelming!), break them down into smaller questions:
   - What activities do you want to learn how to do?
   - What hobbies and activities do you already do, but want to continue doing or get better at?
   - What are your career goals? What steps will need to be accomplished along the way for you to eventually land your dream job? (For example, do you need a particular degree, or will you need to secure an internship?)
   - Do you have relationship goals? Don't think just in terms of whether or not you want to be married, to be in a long-term relationship, or to have children; think more specifically about what kind of person you want to be with, how you'd like to spend time with your partner, etc.
   - How do you want to be remembered by others? For example, do you want to write the next great American novel? Do you want to start or head a charitable/non-profit organization that positively impacts the lives of others?

4. Choose your overriding theme. Based upon the discoveries you've made after completing the above steps, it's now time for you to decide what you want the focus of your Future Lens to be. Don't feel as though you must limit yourself to creating just one Future Lens to reflect all of your dreams. You can make as many separate Future Lenses as you want, each with a different focus.

Now, let's talk about a board with a fairly singular focus:

1. Decide on the format of your Future Lens. Now that you've chosen a theme for your dream board, you'll want to decide the format that it will take. Most people with Future Lenses make physical boards out of poster board, cork board, or on any material that can be hung on or propped against a wall. When it is placed in a prominent position, you'll be able to view your Future Lens regularly and reflect upon it daily.

- However, there's no reason to limit yourself to just this style of Future Lens. You can also make an electronic version of a Future Lens. You can design your own webpage or blog, use sites such as Pinterest, or even just create a private document on your computer, where you'll collect your inspirational images and affirmations.

- Choose the format that you're most comfortable with, and which you'll be most likely to actually look at and update regularly.

2. Collect inspirational images for your Future Lens. Now it's time for you to find positive images that correspond to your chosen theme. Obvious sources are the Internet, magazines, and photographs, but don't forget to keep your eyes open while out and about for funky inspirational postcards, newspaper clippings, labels, etc.

- When choosing your images, select them with a careful eye, making sure to closely examine the entire image.
- For example, if your goal is to get into your dream college, be sure to include an image of the campus, but select shots that are taken during your favorite season or which show students engaged in activities you hope to enjoy while enrolled as a student.

3. Collect inspirational words for your Future Lens. You want your Future Lens to be very visual and to contain plenty of images that appeal to you and which demand your focus. Don't forget, though, to pepper your board with plenty of inspiring sayings or affirmations.

- An affirmation is a positive saying or script that you can repeat to yourself as a mantra. You can of course write your own affirmations, or you can search online for examples or visit your local bookstore or library for inspiration.
- Your aspirations should be positively focused. For example, perhaps your goal is to be selected as first violin in your orchestra; consider something like "I'll fill my home with joyful music daily." This is positive, and makes practicing an activity to look forward to, as opposed to describing it as something to be endured.

4. Put your Future Lens together. Once you've selected your images and inspiring phrases, it's time to get creative with your arrangement. Experiment with different designs—you can find fun examples through online searches, but don't feel as though you have to match anyone else's style.

- Consider choosing a colored background for your Future Lens. Select this color carefully depending on the nature and content of your theme. For example, if you want to stay pumped up about being able to accomplish a difficult physical goal (such as being able to bench press your own weight), choose a strong color, like red.
- If, on the other hand, you are working on achieving peace and calm in your life, choose colors that are soothing, such as a soft blue.
- Think about including a photo of yourself in the center of your Future Lens and surrounding yourself (literally!) with your inspiring images and words.
- Once you've settled on a design and arrangement that appeals to you, secure the components with glue or staples. (If you are making a physical Future Lens, or if you're making an electronic version, be sure to save your file!)

5. Don't be taken in by false promises of what a Future Lens can guarantee. Creating a Future Lens can be a good way for you to find inspiration, identify and shape your dreams, and keep you focused and motivated. If, however, you're thinking about this project because you've heard promises that making a Future Lens is the "right" way, and changing your thinking in the "right" way will guarantee that the universe will deliver what you want—think twice.

- Just be forewarned: there's absolutely no scientific evidence, that by going to the trouble of creating a Future Lens and visualizing your success at achieving your goals, they will automatically happen. If it doesn't, you keep on trying.

- While you shouldn't give up your dreams before you start, understand that life throws roadblocks at you. Sometimes, try as you might, you simply won't be able to achieve everything that you desire. If you go into this project thinking that you'll get results if you do it correctly, and if you then aren't able to get everything you want, you're only setting yourself up for self-blame and disappointment. That can lead to depression or lowered self-worth. So, stay balanced and keep working toward your goals; eventually, the universe will help you.

6. Use your Future Lens to visualize the process, not just the result. Your Future Lens can provide you with a tangible point of focus to help you visualize your goals. However, you should know that there's debate within the scientific community as to how large a role visualizing ought to play in your strategies toward achieving your goals. Recent studies have suggested that people who spend more time visualizing and imagining themselves having obtained success actually underperform once the time comes.

- For example, it has been shown that students who were told to devote time to picturing how swell it would be to do well on a test actually ended up doing worse than those students who were either told to instead visualize their study process or not told anything about visualization relative to the test.
- The lesson to be learned from this and other similar studies seems to be that, while it's good to specify your goals and spend some time envisioning what your life will be like if and when you reach them, it's both more effective and better for your mental

health to focus on the specific steps you'll need to take along the way.
- For example, there's probably nothing wrong with daydreaming about how awesome you'll feel once you cross the finish line of your first marathon. However, you might actually be less likely to ever actually completing the grueling run if all you ever do is visualize this moment of success.
- What time you do spend visualizing would be better spent focused upon your training process. Make sure that your Future Lens has plenty of images and inspirational sayings related to the minutia of training and not just the moment of success. And, of course, don't forget to actually strap on the running shoes and get out there!

For example, your Future Lens might include images of you at a computer; conducting a meeting,;speaking in front of a large audience, discussing bullet points of strategy on a specific document, face to face with a prospect. These will force your mind to focus on the process of writing and speaking and other activities to fulfill your goals.

Write a 'Wikipedic Entry'

As far as I know, I am the inventor of this idea as part of an overall affirmation strategy.

The key here is to write a 'mock' encyclopedic or, in the modern social media world, what I call a 'Wikipedic Entry' or biographical entry that would show up on Wikipedia as yourself.

As Stephen Covey would say in his popular book, *The 7 Habits of Highly Effective People*, "Begin with the end in mind."

Write an entry portraying yourself as successful in your chosen field throughout your life. Include specific accomplishments with prospective dates of each accomplishment.

Dig down deep and think of what it is you want to accomplish in your lifetime, and write it down. Then, prioritize it and start writing in a prose style where it will read as if the events or accomplishments have already happened.

Be careful not to think too magnanimous or too small. Stretch it to include accomplishments with skills you are in the process of acquiring or developing.

Make sure it is only one page in length.

This entry can change as you grow as a person and as a worker. It should be one of the main things you look at first thing in the morning and again last thing at night. The subconscious paints pictures in your dreams that you were thinking about before falling asleep. Better yet, the mind begins to troubleshoot and problem solve while you are sleeping. Effectively, it starts thinking of the ways it can start making some of the things you are thinking about come to pass.

If you read your Wikipedic Entry out loud to yourself before going to sleep, your mind will start to see those events and accomplishments as being real.

The human imagination is a powerful entity that is mostly underused. Use it to your advantage.

Keep in mind every day the importance of being specific with your goals, writing them down, and using the tools of visualization and reinforcement with the recitation of Positive Affirmations.

Use the Power of Positive Music

I know the power of music, having played the drums since age eight and then having sung since about age fifteen.

My father, a fan of classical and jazz, brought me up on music. The Beatles first appeared on *The Ed Sullivan Show* when I was about five. They were a little bit before my 'tween' years; however, by the time I hit my tweens, the Monkees were huge with their TV show.

I started my own band when I was twelve after having taken drum lessons for four years. I played professionally in the Washington, D.C., area even when I was going to college fulltime.

I have spent probably tens of thousands of hours listening to music while driving or while wearing headphones or earbuds. There have been more times than I could count where the music was therapeutic.

Even now as an aging baby boomer, I begin my day with a time of devotion and prayer while listening to inspirational music.

During part of my work career, I have worked in intensive call center environments, where energetic, up-tempo background music was played. It was during that time that I read a newspaper or magazine article that claimed that playing classic rock in a call center actually increased production and sales.

On that Monday morning where you need motivation, put on some energetic music to get you going.

Currently, for relaxation, I listen to a composer named Ulrich Schnauss. He's a former member of a progressive, electronic keyboard-oriented rock music from the eighties named Tangerine Dream. That style now is referred to as electronic ambient, characterized by a drone or a consistent tone playing throughout the music. This characteristic is found in Celtic music from Ireland and also some forms of music found in the Eastern/Asian/Oriental world. The effect is similar to electronic devices that emit 'white noise.' The benefits have been proven, in psychological experiments, to have a soothing effect on the brain and the mind.

Instrumental Western classical music seems to have this effect as well. You might have heard of experiments conducted with plants, in which both classical and hard rock music was played in an arboretum. The plants where classical music was played fared better. However, we did see how, in the example of the call center, the hard rock worked better for participants in a sales environment.

Having been a bandleader in pop music ensembles and a consumer of music, I strongly recommend that when you choose music, choose pieces in which the lyrics are positive. It matters, I assure you. Thoughts and words get into your mind and affect your thinking. God forbid it affects your actions in a negative manner.

At this point in your life or career, you probably have developed your own tastes in music. I encourage you to explore other genres and styles that will help you relax and/or be more productive in your life and work.

Even now, in a coffee shop in the Nashville, Tennessee, area, I find that the overhead music is inspiring me to be most productive in my writing!

Reinforce Ideas Daily

Keep key ideas at the forefront of your mind and reinforce them daily.

Persistence is key in this regard.

Later, I elaborate on the importance of having specific goals and a timeline for their fulfillment.

I also advocate having positive affirmations and a Future Lens to keep yourself on track. It is crucial to keep your targets in sight daily.

Referring to where you are headed and what you want to accomplish in this lifetime will keep you on track. It will also help you avoid distraction and bring about the accomplishment of your desires more quickly.

MINDSETS

7. Mindsets

Have High Expectations

WHAT WE EXPECT TO HAPPEN IN OUR LIVES has a greater chance of occurring than not.

There is a Scripture that I have on my *Biblical Confessions to Build Your Faith* CD (that I use for daily positive self-reinforcement) that says, "That which man fears comes upon him." To be sure, the opposite is true as well.

You have got to get in the mindset and practice to believe that your best days are ahead.

Sometimes I just have to break it down and make a list of what I am thankful for in my life, and keep going from there.

Your leadership opportunities will last longer and be more effective if you reinforce your positive attitude with high expectations. You will be better equipped to fend off the negative reports and general world darkness that surround us from time to time.

Having high expectations is reinforced by having documentation of what you want the future to look like.

In my other chapters, I refer to the Wikipedic Entry, a description of what you want to be remembered for and what you want the rest of your life to look like.

This takes daily discipline. This is why I always advocate that a written version of your expectations exist in laminated form so you can refer to it daily. I keep copies in my portfolio that I keep in my briefcase.

You must have high expectations for health, relationships, vocation, and finances. These are the four major categories of life that consume your time and energy.

Mindsets

If you've ever heard of the Serenity Prayer, you should be familiar with what it says about there being things in your life that you can control and some that you cannot. I am not so naive to think that we can always, magically change circumstance by positive thought. But it can help.

Fact: There are cancer survivors. Doctors know that those with a positive mindset are more likely to recover than those who are pessimistic.

One of my favorite works of psychology is Dr. Maxwell Maltz's *Psycho-Cybernetics*, referenced earlier. In a nutshell, it proposes that there is a cybernetic function in the human brain that is neutral. It acts upon whatever you fill or feed it with. If you see yourself as successful, the brain tells the body how to respond. If you see yourself healthy, then the brain commands the body to react accordingly.

I believe this same phenomenon exists in reality. If you have high expectations of good things coming to pass in your life, they will more than likely tend to occur.

To maintain this mindset takes enormous mental discipline and an ability to bounce back from adversity. To reset one's mind to the positive side of life is an exercise in self-control.

In one of Brian Tracy's motivational seminars, I heard him instruct the audience to say every day, "Something good is going to happen to me today." This is his way of teaching people how to have a high-expectation life. He says that when he recites that, something good almost always does happen in his day.

What have you got to lose? Thinking positively and believing good things can happen to you is a better way to live than thinking and believing negatively.

Sometimes this mindset has to be maintained during

seasons of extended adversity. Hanging on to a positive mindset that things will turn around for the better will almost assuredly bring them about in a shorter period of time.

Anticipate Obstacles . . .

. . . and plan to deal with them in a specific way.

Life is fraught with adversity and distraction. Writing large and smaller-sized attainable goals will help you carry on through the fray. Adversity will be seen more as a nuisance, and you will find yourself urgently working on a solution to get whatever it is out of the way.

When thinking about larger goals, you can almost always think of what it is that could get in your way of fulfillment. In advance, think of ways of how you will deal with those obstacles.

I just watched a video of motivational speaker Larry Winget. He is brutally truthful. He says most people say they are ready to be more successful but they won't do the work it takes to be successful.

One of my closest friends is in the real estate seminar business. He told me a sobering statistic regarding all those who attend, many of whom have the get-rich-quick mentality. He told me only about 10 percent of the attendees will actually follow through with the training. As Winget says, it takes *action*!

Set your goals and *do* them!

Overcoming Adversity

Thick skin and a tender heart. *This* is what it takes to survive and thrive!

The greatest, most influential leaders in history often

have had to overcome great trials. There are four major areas of challenge for humans: health, relationships, vocation, and finance. Almost all of us are challenged in one or more of these areas.

There is no easy answer here. I have experienced setback in all four of these areas, and sometimes the challenge in relationships has left me heartbroken for months or even years at a time.

However, the rent is always due, right? How do you carry on? At a certain point, it becomes necessary to create a wide gap as possible between the personal and business life. As a matter of fact, delving deep into one's work can be a big part of the cure or recovery process.

You will often have to go it alone. Self-destruction is *never* the answer. It is a 24/7 journey sometimes. And the healthiest thing you can do is stay in the game, exercise more, take better care of your body, join social groups, get outside, and help someone else in the same boat or worse. Ever see those homeless people on the street? I once took a college sociology class in which we were taught that about two-thirds of the homeless believe they are getting one over on the system and are sloths/alcoholics, while one-third are mentally incompetent and cannot make good decisions about how to help themselves. These are the ones to have pity on and exercise compassion over. Think of the type of adversity *they* must overcome, and your problems will diminish in scope.

I find that having a life of faith is crucial for me. From time to time I have mentioned that I am a church guy and believe in a higher power. It was instilled in me primarily by a Godly mother, for whom I am eternally grateful. And her father instilled it in her. Many of us have a legacy like that, but many do not. It doesn't matter in the sense that you can develop it on your own and be the first if necessary.

As a leader you are going to face adversity at some point, either in your personal life or in business. Quite possibly both.

The key is to get back up again and keep going. With positive thinking and your written vision, you can get through to the other side.

You are your own best friend and coach. When you're not quite sure, start over, look yourself in the mirror, and give yourself a good talking to. At some point you will have to do it for someone else. A 'street survivor' always makes a greater impact because they have lived through it.

Embrace adversity as opportunity:

- Adversity has made some men and companies great.
- Change your mental paradigm.
- Your response will determine your long-term success.

It is said into every life a little rain must fall. Every day in business, it falls on someone somewhere. It's not whether or not it will happen, but what will be your response to it when it inevitably does.

I prefer to look at adversity as opportunity in disguise.

It might take some time to get through it. It doesn't seem much fun at first; however, there are always lessons to be learned in failure or adversity.

Adversity comes in many forms. It can actually be good for business to have some. Perhaps the competition is upping their game or offering lower prices. Or maybe market conditions are changing.

A perfect example is when Napster entered the market and basically stole songs and offered them for free over the

Mindsets

internet and made money by offering advertising on their site. This is the most common way that media have made money.

Years ago, when I was a broadcasting major at the University of Maryland, I had a professor who said that radio is sales, and sales is radio.

Once this rogue form of spreading music across the Internet reared its ugly head, the recording industry should've rushed in either to control it or make Napster a 'servant' of the business by twisting its arm to insist on payment of royalties.

If the recording companies had seen the handwriting on the wall and not hidden their heads in the sand hoping Napster would go away, they could've retrieved billions in royalties lost to delay. It was actually *opportunity* crashing into the recording and broadcasting world.

The key advantage would've been to change their perception of adversity. If they'd have had their high-powered attorneys confront Napster right away, record companies could've worked out a pay-per-song deal sooner.

In recent years, the retail giant Sears—in some ways the originator of the one-stop-shop concept, now nearly monopolized by Amazon, has been downsizing unable to compete in the Internet economy. Had they had the foresight to see the change and adapt, they might have been able to at least be one of the web's retail leaders. Apparently, leadership was not able to see the change coming and adapt. Subsequently, billions of dollars in revenue were lost as well as thousands of jobs.

Yes, it would've taken massive change and adjustment by Sears and other similar big-box retailers, but there is a popular saying, maybe originating with the Marines that says, "Adapt or die." Reality can be harsh and unmerciful,

73

but in this dog-eat-dog world of business, the prize goes to those who can change and profit from the change.

To embrace adversity as opportunity, you must step back and take an objective analysis of the situation confronting you. Don't wait too long to make some business decisions about what changes need to be made.

Steve Jobs, a genius in many respects, faced some of his greatest adversity after Apple and the Macintosh computers had already changed the computing world and experienced huge success. He had been overruled by a board and stockholders who thought they knew better what direction the company should take. Meanwhile, after a break, he found himself involved with the development of Pixar, the computer graphics company that changed the way films would be made.

He simply was not a soul that would be kept from moving forward.

This is how all leaders must exist and sometimes evolve. When faced with adversity or change, you must grow and try new ideas, conceive new services or improve existing ones, or consider bringing new products to market. You will never know if you are holding the future in your hands until you do.

Avoid Distraction

One key worth revisiting here is to avoid *distraction* from your overall purpose and direction.

I have a college friend who is an outstanding cook in the Creole style popular in Southern Mississippi and Louisiana. We were in the kitchen of a home we were renting once when he profoundly stated that the greatest killer of fine cooking is distraction, meaning foods cooking could be burnt if you aren't paying attention.

Distraction is the enemy of every great achiever. It is so subtle. It is more likely to happen when you tend to procrastinate about achieving goals or you have the fear of failure. The best way to stay focused is to keep reminding yourself of your goals and where you are headed. This comes from having written goals, Positive Affirmations that you listen to or read daily, and having a Future Lens I described earlier.

Avoiding distractions is a skill that must be exercised daily. The discipline to keep oneself on track is priceless.

Distractions come in many forms. How many of you have heard of influential people in positions of authority who see their whole world come crashing down because they were caught in a compromising relationship? We saw this recently in our city of Nashville with the mayor, who ended up resigning after admitting to an affair with one of her staffers.

How did it start? Distraction. Plain and simple. A glance in the wrong direction. A touch. A word.

Distractions always destroy dreams a little bit at a time.

You might have heard it said that 'good' is the enemy of 'best.' This can apply to a decision to take a certain job in a time when funds are running low as opposed to pursuing the ideal career path that might take a little longer to manifest. Years of one's life can be lost in a moment's time from making the wrong decision when distracted.

Be vigilant, be strong, and stay focused while avoiding distraction on what it is you want to accomplish.

The General Upward Direction

Keep the curve moving in a general upward direction.

One of the most powerful principles I ever heard was spoken during a business discussion I was having with one of my former employers, Roy Morgan of Premier Productions in North Carolina. We were talking about business cycles and the longevity of businesses. Roy made the point that, although some businesses experience periodic failures, the main idea is to keep them moving in an upward direction long term.

Brian Tracy describes it another way: You need to get used to the idea of jumping from peak to peak. You acknowledge that there will be downturns in business, but you do not settle there. You deal with the problems and move on to a brighter future of your own choosing.

You begin to view your long-term development as a series of jumps from peak to peak moving in a generally upward direction.

Many investors in the stock market try to look at their portfolio growth as moving from peak to peak. They keep a balance of investments in their portfolio, possibly weighted a little more to the stock side for growth, then they keep their eye on that portfolio through market downturns and upside.

Become Solution-Oriented

It is a huge gift and skill to cut through all the fray and work on solutions.

The marketplace is a tornado swirl of distraction and extraneous information. Negativity and endless complaining and discontent are everywhere.

Mindsets

One of the best things I once heard was about how a leadership consultant went into a corporate culture of negativity and turned it all around. He did this by starting a meeting simply by asking workers if they had an affirmation or recognition for one of their fellow employees. It immediately facilitated an atmosphere of positivity in the room. This is an exercise where proactivity is tantamount. Incorporate the habit of moving toward solutions every time you encounter difficulty or challenge in business, as well as in your personal life for that matter. In doing this, you will build a reputation for being solution-oriented. People will know when they get around you that they will be constantly challenged to participate in discussions of solutions rather than treating this as an opportunity to wallow in a gripe session.

One of the best ways to become solution-oriented is, again, to start writing. Write the problem or challenge you're facing at the top of a blank page. Then start brainstorming solutions without thinking too hard about it. What comes to mind? What pops into your head? Let your brain do the work. Then when you have an exhaustive list, start prioritizing. Eventually, you will come up with the one or two solutions that will work best. It seems simple enough to do it this way, but why make things complicated? Simple solutions are oftentimes the best.

Sometimes it becomes necessary to get away from the problem and think about it. This is what I call Think Time, which I discussed earlier.

Looking at problems and challenges from the top down often helps you see solutions that might not have otherwise been considered. Additionally, becoming a solution-oriented worker means you have to surround yourself with other solution-oriented people. This can be difficult to do if you work with individuals who tend to be negative. Get out of that space as best you can; fire them or have a "come to Jesus" meeting with them. Always do it on an individual basis, never public. The employee will respect you for it.

This radical or forthright way of relating to others can be difficult to maintain. It is not advisable as a mode of operation, but is instead to be used only in scenarios where there is constant moaning and whining about circumstances. We might be exposed to more of this in our personal life, and it might be difficult to get away from, but in the marketplace it should not be tolerated for very long—if at all.

The ideal scenario is to be surrounded by positive-minded, solution-oriented co-workers.

Make it a point to put yourself in the middle of that type of corporate culture.

It is amazing to me how often a corporate culture will emphasize or do the exact opposite and lean away from positivity.

The most influential person is the guy or gal on top. The culture tends to reflect their mindset. This is why as a leader it is crucial to be the difference-maker and set the tone.

Also, conversing with others of a positive mindset, even if they are outside your industry or field, might often reveal good solution ideas because they can see the problem from a different perspective.

Spread some sunshine and be the solution!

THE POWER OF DECISION

8. The Power of Decision

THIS IS SOMETHING MOST FOLKS SHOULD UNDERSTAND; however, it is rarely discussed. It is the single-most-important quality that humans possess over the animal kingdom.

Think of it. It is the one 'switch' you can turn on to move forward, in everything.

A decision is something that has changed the course of human history through time. I grew up in suburban America, where most academically inclined high school students were expected to go to college. I did, although it took me nine and a half years to graduate; I kept making the decision to go back. One semester I even dropped out due to a heartbreak, yet I decided the very next semester to pick myself up and go back. I eventually graduated. Although I probably did it to please my parents, I am sure that my having a degree opened doors several times for me in regard to career development.

I also went through a tough divorce, which could have easily taken me out if I had not had a belief in God and then made a quality decision to get past it and keep moving forward.

Once at a family gathering, a cousin's husband asked me how I dealt with the aging process. Now there's something you don't hear often, but I was prepared. I told him something I read in Og Mandino's *Greatest Salesman in the World*, that I "obey my own command." When something at first seems exhausting to me, to garner my own physical strength, I will count to three. To this day I don't think I have ever 'disobeyed' my own command to move and do what physical task needs to be done on three. Interestingly

The Power of Decision

enough, now there is a movement to count down from five and then move. A bright idea for those of us who have aged, ah well, gracefully I hope.

Try it; it works. 5-4-3-2-1!

If you are ever in a difficult phase of life, you will often find yourself in a position where you have to make a good decision, over and over again. It takes willpower, and, sometimes, all the strength you can muster, but if you value the power of decision and respect it, you will find you are headed down the right path toward your best life possible.

A Leader Must Be a Critical Thinker

There are many skills to master as a leader: critical thinking is one of the most important.

One of the best lessons I ever learned in college was to be a critical thinker. It was from Mrs. Ganz in English 101. One of the reference points she used was how those Germans who remained in Germany during World War II did not stand up to Hitler and his eventual strategy of genocide of the Jews.

Hitler's rise to power was incremental. He preyed upon the people's resentment of how they were left in a difficult place economically after World War I in regard to the treaty of Versailles.

He published *Mein Kampf* and became a public speaker, beginning in the beer halls of Germany. He legitimized the establishment of a political party that condoned the idea of the superiority of an Aryan race. All of it began subtly.

Academics and intellectuals began to leave the country, creating a vacuum of critical thought in the country they abandoned.

One of the only ones to stand up to the spreading of the dark shadow of Nazism was the famous theologian Dietrich Bonhoeffer, who was eventually hanged only a few weeks before the Allies arrived.

Mrs. Ganz's key idea was that to become a critical thinker was to possibly preserve the freedoms enjoyed by Western civilization. If necessary, this was to be done by speaking out against tyranny and oppression. Question everything, she taught us, and look for truth. Assume nothing. In this Internet and social media age, critical thinking becomes that much more important.

At this writing, we live in a world where communism still exists as the form of government in the two other large superpowers (China and Russia) that the United States has to contend with on a daily basis.

Leaders are often in a position where they have to make decisions on their own after considering many different factors and after gaining input from advisors. Critical thinking has to be employed every step of the way.

Leaders in business benefit greatly from critical-thinking ability. A lot of factors go into business decision-making. Information from different sources has to be analyzed and critiqued, although it is not always accurate, as is the case especially with conjecture and opinion.

It has been said that when we are hungry, angry, lonely, or tired, we are more apt to make snap decisions that are not always the best. The key is to be vigilant and always conscientious of the importance of being a critical thinker. Don't let your guard down.

Make it a point not to be swayed in the direction of too much liberal or even conservative media.

Fox News and CNN have their own respective slants. For

The Power of Decision

> the sake of discussion, the *Wall Street Journal* is still one of the last vestiges of objectivity in journalism. The key is that even if you take it all in, you should still question it.
>
> Sometimes in your journey as a critical thinker, you will have to stand against the tide.
>
> There's a saying that I occasionally have to remember, and that is, "The majority ain't necessarily right."
>
> As a matter of fact, sometimes you may have to stand completely alone. It is better to believe you are right in a decision-making process than to go with the crowd just because you want to be accepted.
>
> Critical thinking can save a nation or culture, and it can definitely help you make the best business decisions possible.
>
>

Kill Procrastination

On this particular writing I am practicing what I preach by actually launching into the work of continuing to write this book. Strong, enduring leaders are best at being self-motivated and action-oriented.

    A key component in the business world is the ability to forge ahead despite a desire to stop and rest and accept the status quo.

    One of the major keys is having written goals with a list of possible daily activities directed toward achieving those goals.

    Leaders have to have a certain degree of fortitude to launch into activity when reality is mundane or even, dare I say, depressing.

Personal business can take its toll with relational and/or financial pressures.

Let me say this at this point, that it behooves the individual to have their financial affairs in order so they can keep their minds on tasks that advance larger goals.

One of the best systems I've seen and was ever involved with is Dave Ramsey's "Financial Peace." I was one of his first employees. As a real estate investor caught in a trap of real estate tax law changes beginning in 1986, Dave had to declare bankruptcy before he launched his book writing, publishing, and radio talk show business. Subsequently, he was too broke to pay me. After a month, I had to leave the practice and get my 'real job' back. I was married with our first small child then, so the income stream had to be reliable.

Today, Dave enjoys a more-than-comfortable living. Nearly thirty years after making the effort to reinvent himself following those tough times, Dave now has one thousand team members. He is the perfect example of someone who can prosper after years of perseverance, hard work, and a lot of good decisions.

The value of daily discipline is huge. It must be understood that you should be spending your time on the right thing. This isn't always evident at the beginning of a larger project. There is such a thing as instinct. However, a decision to spend time on something that seems instinctively 'right' should always be substantiated with as many facts and data as possible pointing to eventual success. Do your homework before beginning.

Another motivator, albeit a potentially negative approach, is to think of what your life would be like if you did not pursue your goals. Avoid the 'deathbed' of regret.

The Power of Decision

I am a veteran of the U.S. military, circa the Desert Storm I timeframe (1990-91). Before I went in, I had a fairly effective mode of personal discipline. When I went through Navy bootcamp, I found that they tweaked that discipline. This is the best value of having a military experience. Discipline is a crucial character quality of the leader. Without it, you are less likely to accomplish personal goals, let alone inspire others to stay focused on the accomplishment of organizational goals.

One of the best ways to kill procrastination is to just get started with something small. A start, a beginning of any kind, will make it easier to continue. It is a matter of pushing oneself out of the nest, so to speak.

Self-Discipline: The Master Key

It has been said that the one quality that separates the immensely wealthy and successful people from the mediocre or 'also-rans' is self-discipline. This is the one skill that is emphasized more than any other in military training. In the heat of battle, one needs the ability to think quickly and accurately in order to complete the mission and save lives. The worst decision is the one that is never made, or made too late.

A person's command over their mind and body in terms of self-discipline has more to do with successfully accomplishing something than any other trait does. This trait and skill can be learned. It is a minute-by-minute and step-by-step process.

It is easier to exercise if there is a prescribed duty or deadline. In these instances, a person's main reason to act is probably monetary. If you don't show up and complete the tasks, you don't get paid. If you don't get paid, you end up living on the street.

Self-discipline is more challenging and difficult when there is no prescribed deadline or arrival time.

Anyone entrepreneurial or self-employed knows this all too well.

It also takes self-discipline to educate oneself in subject areas that will bring growth, change, or development.

In the areas of financial services, real estate, or the stock market, it will take a lifetime of learning to master expertise in any one of many areas of knowledge and skill. Mastery will only come about through trial and error. Self-discipline will need to be exercised all along the way.

This is why it is so crucial to have large, overriding goals to help keep oneself focused.

When one is focused on accomplishing a great, long-term dream, it gives impetus to getting up and getting going, to doing whatever it takes to complete a specific project.

I mention entrepreneurs, salesmen, and marketing types because so much of their success depends on repeating a certain process until it becomes mind-numbing.

The faint of heart or those who are slothful usually never see the type of success that can come from the years of repetitive activity required to make headway in business.

For centuries, the benefits of self-discipline in regard to one's personal life have been hailed by many: Eat the right foods, and not too much; exercise; and resist temptation of any kind. Success in those personal areas can spill over into the business world.

Self-discipline is a trait that can be developed through practice. The most important component is desire—I refer to the white-hot desire to be someone who makes a difference, who impacts history, who leaves a personal and financial legacy.

The Power of Decision

A mindset in my own family is to leave an inheritance to one's children's children. To do this, one must be successful in business or one's line of work and wisely manage money. Work to build the goose that lays the golden egg. This is the same concept of annuity that pays a monthly distribution over a lifetime.

The only way to be truly successful at this is to cherish and practice the quality of self-discipline.

Commitment/Stick-to-it-tiveness

Commitment is another character quality that makes a difference. To see something through to the end takes strength and determination. You'll have to be your own best friend and keep talking yourself into keeping your hands on the plow and pushing forward.

Thirteen years ago, I promised myself that I would become a professional speaker and writer . . . and I did just that. I am still in it and plan to be for the duration of my working life.

As I have aged, I have had enough experiences in which I have done a few things that I believed I would like to do, I have arrived at a place where I know this is what I want to do and what I was born to do.

It is this type of assurance that you will need to be committed to your plan for your life. That plan should include a goal of being the best leader that you can be.

You can have the character, the mode of operation, and the understanding of people, but commitment is the key that unlocks your destiny to become what it is you dream about in both your personal and professional life.

Part of what's required to remain committed to a goal or task is the ability to weather the storms that can come against you. Market conditions that go south, low sales, producer or service failures, a glitch in the supply chain, uncooperative co-workers or employees—all those things can contribute to the slowdown of achievement and production.

It's true: When the going gets tough, the tough get going. Another personal favorite of mine, proverbial-wise, is, "When the going gets crazy, the crazy turn professional." They become committed to being excellent at a task or skill.

Difficult or even dangerous circumstances can make commitment an urgent necessity—there is no other choice. The United States in World War II had to be committed to winning the war, regardless. It took Pearl Harbor to wake the sleeping giant (the U.S.). The American people showed great commitment when the war effort involved contributions on so many fronts and at so many levels, not just on the battlefields.

The type of commitment more difficult to muster is when an individual is set to accomplish great things for the benefit of others, directly or indirectly. In such a case a leader has to be self-motivated to remain committed to its completion.

A leader demonstrates commitment to his or her self-development and the people they serve at their company. It can be the quality that makes them a leader in the first place.

In this world of instant gratification, commitment is the exact opposite. It has been said that some people quit just before victory is achieved. The success comes after much toil and struggle and requires the commitment to complete the task or project against all odds. Such is the case with a marathon runner, whose task is to run 26.2 miles—an accomplishment. Win, lose or finish in 500th place, that requires months and months of training leading up to it.

Make it a point to be committed to your own success long-term. It will benefit not only yourself, but also your family, those you work with, and your clients and customers.

You will fulfill what I believe to be the purpose of human existence, and that is to contribute to the lives of others in a positive way.

Sense of Humor

Being a motivational speaker and author, I know full well the value of a sense of humor.

Building a business can be hard, and we need all the comic relief we can get. It is a huge stress reducer. As trainers we know that helpful business information makes a greater impact and is more likely to be retained when humor accompanies it. The most popular and busiest professional speakers in the business are humorists as well.

We can take a clue from television programming. When hard-working Americans come home from work for the evening, they want something to take their minds off the demands of the marketplace. This is why television situational comedies, or sitcoms, predominate the television schedules from 7:00-9:00 P.M. As a quick aside, note how television puts forth policemen and doctors as the heroes of prime time because we all want heroes to look up to. And as a leader, you will have a more productive environment if you are perceived to have 'heroic' qualities. And one of these is being funny or having the ability to see the humor in as many marketplace situations as possible.

One of the best ways to work on or develop a keen sense of humor is to listen to, watch, or read humorous content. In this instance, I recommend taking in as much 'clean comedy' as you can find.

There is, however, little to be gained from what I call bathroom or dirty sex humor or an overuse of verbal expletives. The effect of such low-hanging humor might be immediate because it's considered foreign to everyday 'street level' conversation in business, which is why it will sometimes elicit spontaneous laughter. Such lowbrow humor, however, can come across as an expression of underlying anger or contempt toward a certain situation, and the shock value of the expression will quickly fade. On the other hand, good, solid humor will point to situations where people might be taking themselves too seriously. It will usually take the pressure off a situation. It is never meant to be disrespectful or insulting. One-liners or comments made to be self-deprecating or insulting to another person are not good either. Good, clean humor is hard to find but worth the search.

Many leaders tend to take things too seriously because they are trying to build something worthwhile, such as a good, reputable business. If you have a close friend who has a gift for good humor, strengthen that relationship and learn from them.

In the long run, lighten up some, and you will find yourself and your subordinates to be more fun and productive.

Some of the best clean comedians can be found at thegrablegroup.com, a site operated by a former associate of mine.

DEVELOP THE ENDURING QUALITY OF PERSEVERANCE

9. Develop the Enduring Quality of Perseverance

P ERSEVERANCE IS THE ONE QUALITY THAT SEPARATES champions from also-rans. There must be something deep in the gut or psyche of an individual that keeps them pressing on despite adversity. No one can give it to you. Much of the time it comes from an upbringing in which at least one parent somehow instilled it in you without even being aware they were doing it, yet they must have been modeling perseverance to you.

The individual must possess the ability to see things in the long term or even eternal. The leader must look at his life as making a difference by impacting history.

History has repeatedly shown that those who have impacted our lives in significant ways have likely endured incredible adversity.

TD Jakes, the great minister says, "Great responsibility, great trial." It's as if he's saying that the greater impact you are to have on history, the more trial you will have to endure.

Why is this? It's possibly because the ideas you carry with you will be met with resistance by a larger number of people than if you'd have shared them in smaller circles. Also, your ideas might be cutting against the grain of the status quo.

A good example of someone who persevered is Ray Kroc, the man responsible for expanding McDonald's into an international corporation of fast-food franchises. In *The Founder,* a movie about Kroc's life, his final statement at the end of the movie was that his success could be attributed to perseverance.

Sometimes the adversity is massive. For example, anyone who survived the Holocaust can be considered a superhero.

Develop the Enduring Quality of Perseverance

Anything pertaining to health, relationships, vocation, and finance can be considered extreme. Adversity usually shows up in these four main areas.

I have a motivational CD from Andy Andrews that says in a storm, "The wise and experienced captain keeps his eyes fixed on the lighthouse," to guide his ship safely through the storm to harbor. It is the same way in life. If we have goals and specific accomplishments planned for our lives, by staying focused on those accomplishments, you are more likely to arrive at your desired destination. Another CD I own, *100 Ways to Motivate People* talks about the 'Quit Switch' and how important it is to not flip it.

One of the ways I have survived adversity has been by knowing there was no option other than to carry on. I also have a very strong sense of wanting to accomplish something significant in my lifetime, and I feel like I am nowhere near that, nor do I plan on stopping for what would be considered a traditional retirement. Plus, I don't play golf on a regular basis, nor do I plan to. Aside from trying to exercise my best efforts the majority of the time in my life, I will have to say that the character quality of perseverance has been my most valuable trait. I even had one of my children compliment me on it.

Stay Strong

You not only have to be strong; you also have to stay strong.

The older I get the more I realize life is a marathon. It starts over every day. Inner strength affects all outward signs of strength. Mental and emotional strength can affect your physical strength. Life truly is mind over matter. This is why you must be your own best coach. No one can do it for you.

On my Positive Affirmations CD, which I listen to every day during work commutes, the opening phrase says, "You are the only being in the universe that can cause defeat in your life."

Once you realize you are responsible for achieving your own destiny, your whole outlook will change. You will be empowered to take more action. You will feel stronger with each victory in your life, whether small or large. When you start seeing life as being a finite experience, you will have a better sense of urgency to accomplish the things you set out to do.

Failure's Greatest Teacher

As a fallible human being, I know full well there will be times I will feel defeated or discouraged. The idea is to get back up again and resume going toward your goals. One of the main ideas is to make sure these 'down' times get shorter in length.

In regard to inventing the electric light bulb, Thomas Edison said that, for the thousands of experiments that didn't work, he never failed, he "just found out a few thousand ways that didn't work." (Interestingly enough, the 'vacuum factor' in the bulb is what made the difference.)

Many motivational teachers endorse the approach that failure is the only way to success. People who have impacted history or made any kind of significant headway in ordinary life have likely found that the more failures you have, the closer you are to success.

If we take Edison's view that we just found some ways that didn't work, we can move on without too much depression to try, try again.

After returning to the speaking business, I tried to

Develop the Enduring Quality of Perseverance

jumpstart it with some retirement seminars. My friend recommended that I try three test markets. I had rooms reserved, mailings printed and sent, and what I thought were some decent workbooks printed.

Unfortunately, the seminars turned out to be dismal failures, and I lost several thousand dollars. I learned a lot, though. I learned that I needed to be better prepared and to begin promoting the events much further out.

Since I had no option but to continue on, I did.

I also learned that I needed to stick to my core topics that had earlier brought me some success: motivation and leadership training.

I also decided to get on with it and write this book, developing outlines and notes I had kept for more than twenty years.

I have also experienced failure in other areas of my personal life. What I have found is that I must've been born with a 'carry on' gene—the ability to keep going in spite of letdowns involving people, business, or other circumstances.

One of my hero role models is Abraham Lincoln. He endured enormous adversities and lost numerous elections before he was elected president of the United States. He endured painful personal tragedy, having lost a son to illness and being in a marriage with Mary Todd, who struggled with terrible depression and was probably bipolar.

Lincoln had political enemies who made his policies difficult to pass into legislation. He endured, however, and saved the Union, only for his life to be cut short by an assassin.

All the while, Lincoln held onto to a strong faith in God and a sense that he had a purpose. He held on to principles that he had carried with him since childhood, and he attributes much of his force of personality to a strong mother and what she taught him about life.

Many high achievers have mentioned that they had a role model or mentor whom they looked up to and admired while following the principles taught to them.

Most of those people who endure and accomplish great things have this sense of destiny and purpose. It's the thing that carries them through long-term. Failures are seen as nothing but a bump in the road. The real secret is to learn everything you can from the failure and to not repeat the same mistakes. This, too, is part of the formula for success.

And in Churchill's words, "Never, Never, Never Quit!"

This Too Shall Pass

This is a principle often heard among those familiar with twelve-step programs, but it is a powerful truth nonetheless: This too shall pass.

It is a phrase to keep in the back of your mind as a source of comfort when things go wrong, as they sometimes will. If things happen in business that are not the end of the world, such as losing a bunch of money on a bad deal or getting fired for doing something really stupid, then accept the reality that the wheel goes 'round and once things settle down, you can get back to the grindstone and keep pushing forward.

Success comes and goes. The economy does well for a while and then inevitably runs into trouble. It happens. Still we keep working, making things happen, living our lives, falling in and out of love, raising children, etc.

When the going gets tough, the tough get going, right? If you have lived long enough, you know that change is inevitable. To a large degree it is comforting to know that the

Develop the Enduring Quality of Perseverance

wheel of life goes around, and things inevitably get better after they get worse.

The same is true of success. Fame and glory are fleeting, too. It's like lightning across the sky, borrowing from the lyrics of a song by the Canadian band Rush.

Keep this idea in your back pocket, and you will have a better understanding of one of life's great truths, that this, too, shall pass. For better or worse.

Success Breeds Success: The Snowball Effect

I realize I am reaching both leaders who have been in those positions for a while and those who might be new to it. Generally, my best guess is that your leadership abilities have been developing since childhood.

A welcoming fact about the marketplace is that the longer you have been exercising your leadership abilities, the more success you've encountered, provided that you have been growing as a leader. Or maybe there are reasons you are digging for good information on leadership.

In any case, I hope things are going well for you. Be assured, as you experience more success as a leader, that the universe has a way of tracking you down and offering greater opportunity and even more success. It has a snowball effect.

Be careful of the pride that might come and then puff you up to where you act as if you did it all by yourself.

One major characteristic of leadership success is that there were probably several good people that helped you get there. Don't let them down. Give credit where credit is due.

I just happen to be writing this part of the book on Administrative Professionals Day in America. My wife received a nice card and a flower and a gift card from her company's leadership. Good administrators are worth rewarding. Their work is invaluable to a leader's success.

Stay diligent, stay strong, and keep working with the utmost effectiveness. Take the human factor into account when leading your people, and success will track you down. That snowball will keep getting bigger as it rolls down the hill.

Finish Strong!

It has less to do with how you begin and more to do with how you end up. I believe strongly in people trying to start over or take their lives to another level.

If you feel lost in a sea of negative or mundane circumstances, you are never too old to reassess and get back on track toward making your dreams/goals come true.

One of the most inspiring stories I ever read while in college was of a senior woman who had a dream of playing in the New York City Symphony. She was sixty years old. In pursuit of her dream, she buckled down, took cello lessons, practiced hard for five years, and then auditioned and got a position with the Symphony.

It's never too late, unless you're dead!

So get on it and get back to basics; get on with your plan to make your life better! Get a written plan going and work it.

Daily discipline is key as are written reminders to yourself as to where you are headed and how you are going to get there.

The struggle can be difficult and the road seem long. Naysayers and doubters are a dime a dozen. Nothing they have to say matters. Being true to self is a huge part of this.

Develop the Enduring Quality of Perseverance

Wake up every morning with a rededication to your strategy and move forward.

I want to be especially encouraging to those of you who are working a dead-end job but have a plan for improvement. Maybe you are having to work two jobs to pay bills. I encourage you to use every spare moment to work on your dream. It can be done. Thousands before you have accomplished it. You can be one of those, victorious at the end of your struggle, to say, "It was hard but I did it, and it was worth it." Think of the many others you will inspire to go the distance as well. That in itself can motivate you and encourage you along the way.

BECOME A MASTER COMMUNICATOR

10. Become a Master Communicator

Effectively communicate a clear vision. Inspire and motivate! Start by mastering the five keys below (these will keep you plenty busy and motivated for a while):
- Become a powerful business writer.
- Be a great listener.
- Present effectively face to face.
- Communicate effectively in the social media environment.
- Communicate effectively on the telephone, talking and persuading.

Become a public presenter.

Becoming a great communicator is almost as important as having strong people skills.

Ronald Reagan was dubbed "the Great Communicator" because he had the ability to encourage and motivate the American public in the 1980s, which turned out to be a time of economic prosperity.

Listening is the most important communication skill of all. This is something I have to work on regularly. Some of us Type A's who have a plan and an agenda tend to give our own ideas top (and sole) priority, even when those with whom we work can also have valuable input. We talk over them or look for openings in the discussion or conversation to talk about our ideas first or devalue what others might have to contribute. Those of us who do this must learn to stop, shut up, and listen. Many of us must proactively train ourselves on a case-by-case basis. It is a weakness that must be overcome. We should give it as much priority as our overall business success.

Become a Master Communicator

Great leaders usually start out being great face-to-face communicators while in childhood. They learned how to rally the children together to play a game of ball or tag or some other group game. They often become leaders in sales at a young age. For some of us in the pre-social media world, this skill was transferred to the telephone.

Did you know that the telephone is still the most powerful business tool in the marketplace? Its communication requires a response, whereas an email, text, or social media advertising can be ignored.

When the chips are down, a major decision or success in high-level negotiations often will depend on smart use of the telephone.

It is also imperative that the leader develop outstanding face-to-face communication skills. One of the key skills required in face-to-face negotiating is not the ability to persuade the other party to endorse your view of the matter being discussed or product or service being sold; it is to listen to the other person's concerns or interests. Listening carefully and patiently to the other party's point of view allows you to generate an appropriate response that will most likely persuade the other party to buy into your line of reasoning. Or they might even present a solution or scenario that is even more beneficial to all parties concerned, perhaps something you hadn't even thought about. Accept the fact that you don't always have all the best answers or solutions.

Listen! and then respond.

Unfortunately, most salespeople are so interested in telling their story that they completely ride roughshod over the other person's concerns, or they don't ever find out if the other party really has any interest.

This ability to listen and persuade can be transferred to

the use of the phone for business purposes. The need to listen is especially important here because it's all you have—as opposed to face-to-face, when you can read body language and facial expressions.

Then there's business *writing*. In this digital age, the ability to communicate effectively in an email is mandatory. That mode of operation has even gone a step further to include texting.

Many leaders have learned through trial and error what constitutes a clear, understandable, and, in some cases, persuasive email.

One of the keys to good communication in the digital age is to be clean of any profane, rude, negative, or humanly prejudicial statements or photos. Early on, you might have been able to get away with some of that stuff, but now you want to abide by the old rule of, "If it isn't something you would print on the front page of *The New York Times*, then you probably don't want to print (post) it."

The effective leader must take it a step further and become a powerful and clear business writer in regard to writing business reports and proposals.

These communication skills require that a person have the ability to think clearly and logically.

A leader must have an organized mind. I'm talking about *you*. You must develop the ability to organize thoughts in your head. Major ideas have to be followed by minor ideas. Think of it as an outline, but one that is imprinted on your mind. I find that consistent reading activity helps me to do this competently.

Like I mentioned earlier, I have a reading list of books, listed according to topic, that I have lined up and organized in a book basket by my evening reading chair. I devote at

Become a Master Communicator

least an hour or two to reading in the evening.

Reading is a more valuable activity than watching television. It puts your mind to work, thinking about the information and processing it.

If you need to improve your leadership communication skills, there are great books on those topics. Get one and dive into it today!

Ultimately, a great leader will want to become an outstanding and effective public presenter.

When building a team or an effective enterprise, you will need to address large and small groups. It's important to note that nations have been swayed by powerful speakers, in both positive and negative ways. Public speaking is a powerful tool.

To hone and polish your speaking skills—in the process boosting your confidence level as well—I recommend membership in the best local Toastmasters club you can find. It is the very organization where I learned to develop my professional speaking skills.

Crash through the wall of the fear of public speaking. Once you get the hang of it, you'll find it to be one of the most effective ways of sharing your ideas.

Effectively Communicate a Clear Vision

There is a verse in the Bible that says, "Without vision, the people perish." Whether you are religious or not, the principle still holds true. A company or organization needs a bigger picture purpose or goal to shoot for to make it successful.

I like what Brian Tracy says in his YouTube video on *Secrets of Self-Made Millionaires*; he encourages the observer/listener to, "Dream big dreams!" I, for one, am in total agreement. As a matter of fact, I was just looking at

Facebook, which I actually try not to do very often (lol), and someone had posted a short video on the life of Tesla. He's the great innovative scientist/engineer (a rival of Edison's, no less), whose bottom-line philosophy was that all advancement in science and technology should be done to benefit mankind. His concepts were enormous and futuristic. Without going into detail regarding his work (it is worth it to investigate it on your own), the main issue is that most people are probably working far below their potential.

Tesla impacted world history by encouraging men to build an alternating current electrical system instead of direct current as Edison and others would've liked.

Another proverbial statement I like (obviously, because I repeat it here): "It is better to shoot for the moon and hit the eagle than shoot for the eagle and only hit a rock."

I always encourage people to dream as big as they want to. I even have goals and ideas for certain work that I have written down in private writings because I know they are magnanimous and would seem impossible to some.

One key idea in business is to have a large 'doable' vision—one that would be realistically possible in the long term. It should be written down as specifically or in as much detail as possible.

Some of this comes in the form of having a written business plan.

In the section immediately preceding this one, I discuss how important it is for a leader to have masterful communication skills. Once the larger vision is in some written, visible form, it must be properly and effectively communicated by its originator or by someone closely associated with the originator who is a masterful communicator.

Become a Master Communicator

It helps to have reminders or even visuals around the inside of an office building, warehouse, or factory—whatever your work setting might be—of the larger vision for workers to see and think about while they are turning production.

I know of a church here in the Nashville, Tennessee, market that does this. Very specific principles reminding the people of the founding pastor's main teaching ideas are posted on the walls of the inside of the church. He refers to them often in his sermons as well. No confusion here. The people know exactly where their pastor is coming from and what he wants them to believe.

All constructive activity should be based on a larger vision or concepts.

Pictures and words are powerful, especially when they are combined in some way.

Earlier, I described the power of having a Future Lens and "brainwashing" yourself with powerful positive affirmations of who you are and what you are born to accomplish. Much of this I do at the first part of the day to set my own direction.

There's also the Wikipedic Entry as I described earlier. With this in hand, I have effectively communicated a clear vision to myself of what I am to be doing with my time in making my dream a reality.

My charge to all business owners, managers, and leaders is to have a clear vision with specific direction as to how it's going to get done and to communicate it to those who will help make the dream a reality.

MANAGING OTHERS

11. Managing Others

Leadership Is Influence

ONE OF JOHN MAXWELL'S KEY PRINCIPLES IS that leadership is influence. He tells a story about when he first started pastoring at a small rural church in Indiana, where a farmer named Claude had been leading the people at church board meetings for years. Maxwell wisely deferred to this scenario. He was not about to rock the board of the established order. Instead, Maxwell recruited Claude's friendship and ran ideas past him because he knew he would be presenting them at the next board meeting.

Instead of being heavy-handed and insisting on his own way, John wisely discerned that Claude's influence had been present at the church for years. The best-case scenario was to win Claude's trust and continue with the way things got done at the church.

Claude always seemed to be a 'good ol' boy,' and he sincerely cared about the welfare of the church. The other side of this is, if Claude had been a negative influence, it would've been necessary to change the way things got done and proactively try to influence the board members to see things differently. Fortunately, for Maxwell, he didn't have to take that latter approach.

This brings me to an important concept, that leadership can be positive or negative influence. Extreme examples in history point to monsters like Hitler or Stalin, who massacred millions of their own people due to paranoia and hatred.

Influence can be gained over time. It usually comes from your being in a position of speaking your mind or in a position of visibility (or both, for that matter).

Managing Others

Being in a position of influence can determine the outcome of elections, as well as the future of companies and organizations.

Leaders sometimes gain influence by being the most vocal entity within an organization. However, in doing so, they have to prove to everyone that they are always accurate in their evaluation of a certain situation in terms of advancing the goals of the organization or improving marketing or sales efforts.

If a leader wants influence in an organization, it is going to require good communication skills and a basic understanding of how things get done in the organization. Ultimately, those in the organization navigate for them.

Maxwell also says leaders who become influential "enlarge" people, or make them feel good about themselves and help them grow. They connect with people and empower them. They will eventually hand off more responsibility. I once heard it said that the one quality in a leader that workers like most is not micromanaging them.

This is beneficial if a worker can be trusted to produce. In such instances, the best mode of operation for production is to avoid having workers 'clock in' to perform tasks; instead, give them an assignment and the tools to complete the production, letting them ply their skills to produce in an environment of trust.

Most importantly, leaders with influence create other leaders who are in turn able to reproduce other leaders themselves. On and on it goes.

The most influential leaders set an example for others in the type of work that is to be performed, then they trust others to do the work required with excellence and a servant's attitude toward the client or customer.

Master Human Psychology

You must love people and become a master of human psychology.

Managing people this way is a tough assignment, and it will take everything you've got to make this a daily habit. Also, your life experiences will influence your approach to this as well. For example, what your parents were like, your upbringing, sibling relationships, love relationships (including betrayals, divorces, etc.) will all influence you.

In a nutshell, *forgiveness* is the only thing that will save you from a world of hurt and being held back by bitterness, etc. There are some who will have to be forgiven a thousand times (and this works both ways). I know . . . I have lived it, personally.

Because some people tend to be misanthropic, this will take a very specific effort on the part of some to do it—loving people, that is.

I ultimately believe that every human being is born with a clean slate and is taught ways of relating (good or bad) primarily in their early years of upbringing. I try to let people be themselves in the sense that I am constantly moving toward a position of being nonjudgmental.

People make mistakes. I certainly have; haven't you? It is those people who try to correct those mistakes made in relationships, or to at least make amends and reconcile, who deserve a second chance.

So, if you are going to manage people or build an enterprise, you will have to love people, flaws and all. This is *not* in defense of the wicked or evil persons who *choose* to hurt or even kill others.

I am talking about dealing with the public in the general marketplace.

Managing Others

How do you become a master of human psychology? One way to do so is to understand the four major personality types: The Driver or type A's, the Socialites, the Perfectionistic Melancholies, and the Phlegmatics or Peacekeepers. Each of these personalities requires a different approach in order to be managed. Drivers are typically motivated by money or status. Socialites are most concerned with the condition of their relationships and having *fun*. Melancholies like order, cleanliness, and *accuracy*. Phlegmatics just like it when everyone gets along and strives to bring cooperation and tolerance. To some degree, people skills can take you further in life than any technical or creative skill.

> **Develop a System of Accountability**
>
> Having a system of accountability is especially important, (*e.g.* when you are building a long-term plan). This is crucial if you are multitalented; the more people you have keeping track of your progress or your adherence to your goals, the better.
>
> It is not necessarily best for you if your accountability partners are parents, employers, or others who are in an official supervisory or authoritative role in your life. This type of accountability role is better suited to close friends, those you can trust. The operative term here is *trust*. You will want this to be someone who will never air your 'dirty laundry.' Trustworthy individuals like this are few and far between.
>
> Essentially, you will have to see the value in having an accountability partner yourself.
>
> Touching base with your accountability partner once a month or every six weeks should suffice. A phone call should do, but a face-to-face meeting over coffee or lunch is preferred.

> This person should be familiar or briefed on your overriding goals to the point where they can ask you point blank how you're doing on them.
>
> Part of the benefit of having an accountability partner is that if you know you have someone to ask you how you're doing. This will help you stay on task.
>
> A footnote to those of you who are married: Husbands: It is always best to get feedback and support from your wives. God put them in your life to verify direction and sometimes to make adjustment. Wives: You must pray for your husbands that he will find the perfect way.
>
>

Connectivity

One of the most important principles of leadership is the cold hard fact that you must love people. It is the hardest thing to do, yet it must be done.

The first place to start is in front of the mirror. How you treat yourself is probably how you will treat others. You will need a very thick skin, and you will need to be quick to forgive and to generally overlook the faults and failures of others.

In the professional realm, of course, a certain corporate code of behavior is expected. So, to some degree, it is easier to manage people in this arena than it is to manage family and friends in your personal life.

To be an effective leader you will need to connect at some point. This is a quality difficult to quantify. It is one of those experiences where you can just tell if it's happening or not.

Managing Others

You will especially want this 'connection' if you are going to be managing salespeople.

Sales is challenging, hard work. It gets even more so if the stakes are high and the price of products or services is generally higher than the competition's. In order for you to be able to help your people, connection is necessary because you will sometimes need to help them get over the hump. That's a challenge they might be having, even when you know they are talented and really trying. You might need to pull them up out of a slump. To have the most effective influence and persuasive impact on struggling yet sincere salespeople, you will have to have the type of personality that they believe in. They must trust and believe that you have their best interests in mind and that you truly want to see them succeed.

Understand People

To best understand people, you will also need to educate yourself on how personality theory works. I touched on that a little bit back, referring to the drivers, the social butterflies, the perfectionists, and the peacemakers.

In sales you get mostly drivers and socialites. Drivers will be motivated by the numbers, and socialites will basically just enjoy being around people. Sales managers find those types to generally be easier to manage. The peacemaker, however, might just be too nice and not driven enough, while perfectionists can get lost in detail and never get to closing the sale.

Each personality type will have hot buttons or best ways to be motivated. The longer you work with people, the better you will understand them.

Some people are more fit to lead than others. I believe

all people are born to lead; whether or not they get there depends on if their leadership skills are developed.

People are the most valuable resource we have in this life. Land and capital are usually the other two elements that combine with labor to create an economy. If you get right down to it, people are the valuable resources needed to secure land and capital goods. If you connect with people, the other factors fall into place.

J. Paul Getty was one of America's most powerful oil barons of the twentieth century. He said his secret was not that he knew everything about the oil business, but that he did know how to assemble a team of people who were the best at what they did in the business. His strength was in recruiting. Then he made it a point to lead that team. We can assume that he was able to persuade these talented and skilled people because he genuinely had good people skills.

A misanthrope can use all the excuses available to explain why he is not successful or why his organization is failing; however, it can all be traced back to people skills.

One of the ways you can overcome a scenario where people are difficult to work with is to draw a line down the middle of a page. On one side list their positive qualities; on the other, list their negative characteristics. Then, in your next management scenario in which that person is involved, focus on the positive and appeal to their better side; motivate them to focus on their strengths, and see how that goes.

The basic stance of liking and trusting people is the single greatest contributor to business success. This is why the socializer might be the most successful in a business sense despite being only marginally talented and skilled. People just like working with someone who likes them.

Make it a point to be good and kind to people even if

you must manage with a steel fist in a velvet glove periodically. You will like the results.

Personality Magnetism

Not every leader will have a magnetic personality, although it is not really a requirement, per se. A smile, though, goes a long way—it can have a huge positive effect on people.

I have listened to Andy Andrews's *7 Decisions for Success* for a few years now. One of its components is his advocacy for having a smile. Ever since I heard it, I've been trying to do it. A smile is especially effective in a retail environment, where many service workers such as wait staff and cashiers have tough jobs and probably are not paid what they are worth. It's amazing how their faces can light up when you give them a smile and show them a little kindness.

My dear mother used to smile as a matter of habit. I did not realize how powerful it was until I started exercising the practice on purpose.

Other factors that compose a personality that endears subordinates to you include good grooming and sanitary practices (a daily shower, for starters, complete with deodorant). I will not say much on this, but if you can avoid getting or having tattoos, please do so. Not only will tattoos be a sight when you are older, but if they are pronounced and evident on a part of the body not covered by clothing, they might even be a deterrent to getting a decent job or making a good impression on a potential customer or client when face to face.

Do whatever it takes to have some joy in your life. I fully recognize that we all go through seasons of difficulty; however, the idea is to quickly bounce back. Make sure you are in a job where you are doing what you love or it at least uses some of your stronger skill sets while you are working your way to a job you love. Vocational satisfaction is a huge contributor to overall happiness.

This happiness is exuded in one's demeanor and another contributing factor to that desirable magnetic personality.

There is a saying in the sales world that people buy from those they know, like, and trust. Strive to be that person. You should also know your products well and be prepared to answer tough questions regarding their content and/or function. In many instances, the salesperson with some basic knowledge but a very likable personality will find success more readily than a thoroughly knowledgeable salesperson with a stoic or static demeanor.

If you do not feel that your personality is magnetic to begin with, make yourself magnetic by being aware of some of these principles and employing them.

Keep a Healthy Distance

Sometimes this principle of keeping subordinates at more than arm's length doesn't make sense, but the U.S. military employs it. In the long term, being too close to subordinates breeds unhealthy familiarity and eventually a lack of respect. An individual might think that because they have an inside track to a leader, it gives them the right to question the authority of that leader.

An atmosphere where a select few have 'special' access to the leader can create animosity and contempt for both leaders and associates. Don't get too chummy with your subordinates.

And I must say it here: Do not avail yourself of a sexual relationship with a subordinate or engage in sexual harassment. Either is a career destroyer and possibly a 'lifedestroyer.'

Managing Others

A worst-case scenario in this regard can bring on such stress as to result in utter social humiliation and embarrassment. It could quite possibly lead to self-destruction or slow suicide through excess use of alcohol or worse, pill and/or drug addiction.

Marijuana use is particularly deceiving. The problem with drug use is that it might seem pleasurable at the outset, but progressively it gets worse, leading to lethargy, inordinate desire, and a compromise of inherent values such as honesty.

Advocating this drawing of lines of authority is not meant to be "mean," it's only to contribute to the health and productivity of the organization or team.

If you engage in an equal or close relationship with a subordinate and you find yourself giving priority to it, you might be forced to choose between a job and a romance. Keep your head on straight and think logically by removing the emotional dimension when making *major* decisions in this regard. This is probably why some companies/organizations discourage nepotism or the hiring of family and relatives.

The main idea here is to separate business from pleasure.

As a young person, I became a professional musician at an early age (twelve). In groups with a combination of genders, especially if the front person or main lead singer is a female in a group otherwise comprised of men, there can be the temptation and tendency to sleep with the girl/young woman. A couple of older, more seasoned veteran players I worked with described it as, "You wouldn't cook something in your bathroom or (defecate) in the kitchen, would you?"

They made their point, and it made a huge difference for me in the years to come. Keep business separate from pleasure, and vice versa, and, as I mentioned in an earlier chapter, maintain life balance.

A Steel Fist in a Velvet Glove

The general idea of leading or managing people in this manner is to maintain that idea of loving people but still being firm in holding them accountable. In cases where production or efficiency is slipping, you might have to motivate subordinates to get back on track to do their job. In rare circumstances, you might have to fire someone, preferably after three warnings. This is in order to give them the benefit of the doubt and allow the subordinates to manage themselves and refocus back to self-improvement.

As in our previous discussion of how the four major personalities need to be managed differently and are motivated by different factors, you will sometimes have to call a subordinate "on the carpet." However, do *not* ever reprimand a subordinate in public. Do it privately. They will respect you for it by not embarrassing them in front of their peers.

Firing people is hard.

I heard it said that the first time you think of firing an employee is when you should do it. In cases where you want to exercise compassion, here are some guidelines:

- If a subordinate seems to be struggling with personal issues, such as a problem with a relationship or drinking alcohol in excess or substance abuse, give them an opportunity to fix it. Suggest a twelve-step program or counseling. If the problem persists, you will have to exercise 'tough love' and let them go for the sake of the health of the organization.
- If it has to do with a general lack of focus, discuss it with the subordinate in detail. Give them room to breathe, yet set boundaries and requirements for improvement with specific time deadlines. If they show

no improvement in performance after three warnings or meetings, let them go. People almost always fire themselves through bad behavior or low production. This is especially difficult if the subordinate has had a track record of good production. People change. Circumstances change. It is your responsibility to keep the organization moving forward and preferably growing exponentially. Cast off dead weight.

Subordinates can get distracted if they become unhappy in their work, especially if they are considering a job change or are being recruited by a competitor. Disloyalty has already set in and probably will never be resolved. Cut the cancer out before it spreads. You have no idea what kind of off-the-record conversations are taking place with associates or even what kind of proprietary information is being shared with this employee's future employer.

In rare cases where the individual is *extremely* talented or valuable, you need to decide if you should try to retain the employee by sweetening the pot—it might not be worth it. Even if you get them to stay, they have already shown you once they are willing to leave you in a lurch by jumping to another job, and chances are they will do it again three months, six months, etc. later. Cross that bridge when you get there and do not kowtow or grovel or promise them the moon. Check the source; they might be bluffing.

Treat Subordinates as Individuals, Not Numbers

Legendary rocker Bob Seger had a hit song called "Feel Like a Number." I think of that song when touching on this subject of treating people like individual humans instead of as numbers.

In this digital age of information overload and social media, it's easy for people to get stuck and feel like they are not appreciated for their individuality. In fact, in the ingenious system of U.S. military boot camp, they employ a strategy (eight weeks in my case) of "grinding to powder" the individuality of a recruit to build a unified fighting force, a team whose lives might depend on each other in life-threatening warfare. Then just when they have "congealed" recruits into a team, they spend the last several weeks building up recruits to make them feel like they are the greatest warriors on the planet.

A different dynamic exists in the business marketplace. It is absolutely crucial that you manage subordinates one on one, respecting the uniqueness of the individual.

Look past the person sitting across the desk from you. This is someone who grew up somewhere within the context of a particular culture (likely different from yours), raised by parents with a set of personalities, presumably with siblings in a certain birth order (this, in and of itself, can determine a person's response to leadership). For example, the oldest child and the youngest child can become natural-born leaders due to the fact that the oldest is responsible for setting the example and the youngest is often coddled by the mother or caregiving parent to develop a sense of self-confidence. Middle children are often the 'peacemakers' in a family.

I believe all human beings are valuable. Even the wicked and criminal did not start out that way. Something happened in their lifetime or upbringing that shaped their experience and decision making. I am *not* making excuses for repeat offenders, but sometimes, given second chances and the right guidance and influences, these individuals can do a 180-degree turnabout. It does happen. Only those who show no sign of change should bear the punishment tied to their offense(s).

This type of extreme negative behavior is not usually present in corporate culture unless it has gone undetected only to be eventually discovered in such cases as white-collar crime. This can now be seen in the Information Age in terms of hackers and those who maliciously destroy or damage irreparably the information systems so crucial to the smooth day-to-day operation of government and business.

Here's a principle I like: "Believe the best unless proven otherwise."

People have home lives, spouses, children, extended family, possibly aging parents. Cut them some slack, but draw boundaries.

Add Value to Others

In Brian Tracy's *Psychology of Achievement*, he mentions the Law of Expectation, where events or accomplishments are more likely to happen in your life the way you expect them to.

He points out that this is also true in relationships. A good leader who expects the best performance from his people will more than likely get it because it is human nature to rise to the levels of expectations that are put on them.

Ultimately, we can add value to people when we expect the best from them. When we are constantly referring to and expressing appreciation of their strengths, we will find that those strengths become more prevalent.

Likewise, a negative leader who expects that people will perform at their worst will probably get that level of performance.

When a leader inherits a team from another leader, be it in positive or negative circumstances, they will have to assess whether or not the predecessor expected that team to perform at their best, mediocre, or worse, or just didn't care. They will have to take the time and involvement to set the new standard and see if the people will come up to a new level.

They will have to give such expected change a deadline to see if the performance improves or deteriorates. Over time, individuals might need to be singled out for added training or even termination. Before that, there might be a need to encourage them in their strengths. However, if for whatever reason a particular team member does not perform up to a certain level of positive expectation, they might have to be let go.

It is always in the best interest of the company to add value to employees by providing them with leadership that will impart a vision and a sense of direction as well as positive reinforcement.

It is from constant encouragement and positive expectation that employees perform to the best of their ability. Giving them the benefit of the doubt at first will increase the chances for success in the overall operation of the division or the enterprise.

Conflict Resolution

As a leader, you will occasionally encounter scenarios where you need to resolve conflict with a subordinate. One bit of key advice: Don't let the issue(s) involved build up in a pressure cooker. Address issues of concern earlier rather than later. Don't get so angry that you just start blowing up at someone—that never works. It only causes

Managing Others

the employee in question to throw up defenses and push back.

The best approach is to ask questions and listen. Gauge the general feeling of the employee's level of satisfaction about the job from them. Are they even happy there overall, or is it a more isolated scenario that can be addressed and solved with some cooperation and agreement? Obviously, the latter scenario is a better situation to have. Otherwise, you might find yourself in a situation that is going to take more time and involve bigger decisions.

In every instance whenever possible, listen to the employee to get how they feel about how a problem can get resolved. Their solution might be better than whatever you had in mind. If their suggestion is feasible and affordable for the company or organization, and if they feel like they can implement the strategy, it might be best to let them move forward with it. Give it a shot at least. Otherwise, you can offer alternative solutions that are within the framework of their responsibility.

If you have issues of teamwork or whether someone is getting along with coworkers, do not bring them in one by one. Bring them in together so they can come to their own solutions about how to better work together or not. You might have to let one go if the disturbance is detrimental to the team. In this instance, you might have to go with your gut; however, still give yourself at least an hour to think about it—after they both have left the room.

If you have an employee who is frequently coming to you with problems, at some point you are going to have to be firm with them and coach them on how to solve many of their problems on their own.

In each case, if you are trying your best to be a good

manager and are setting a good example workwise—and if they know, like, and trust you—you are going to have the influence on them to do the same.

You will sometimes have a company policy or policies that need to be adhered to, but in many cases you will have some wiggle room.

I always like to work with a 1-2-3 strikes—"you're out"—method in regard to whether or not to keep an employee with low production, poor performance, or multiple policy infractions.

It is most fair in most cases to give the employee the benefit of the doubt first and let them first come up with their own resolution to a problem or be willing to employ yours with a checkup or revisit in two weeks to ninety days depending upon the scenario.

In most cases it is always best to exhaust every possible solution to a problem, but give it a deadline. Action will have to be taken or there comes a tipping point.

We live in such a fast-paced, competitive marketplace that making decisions in a timely manner in one form or another is necessary to maintain the profitability of the enterprise.

People are people, and that means things can get messy sometimes. If you are communicating a clear vision and people are willing to follow it, you are going to have to periodically gauge the buy-in.

The ship may change directions at times, but generally you are going to want to have people on board who believe in the mission and the purpose of the products or services offered. If that changes within even just a microcosm of the company, it needs to be addressed and resolved in a timely manner. Yet it must be carried out with as much empathy as can be afforded, and always with a solution-oriented mode of operation.

Make sure to focus on solving the problem and not attacking the people within an organization.

LEADERSHIP PRACTICES

12. Leadership Practices

Trust Brings Respect

WHEN A LEADER TRUSTS HIS EMPLOYEES TO DO their best, they will perform to the best of their ability. Employees rise to the level of expectations put on them. When this type of environment exists, employees will respect their leaders.

Employee respect should be one of your highest goals as a leader. When you trust them to do their best work on a daily basis and you earn their respect along the way, you will see levels of production go through the roof.

How is trust earned? It is earned by being a leader whose words and actions are in sync. It is earned by being a leader who knows what direction the entire company is taking and what his division's role is in the overall vision of the company.

A leader who sets the bar a little higher than what he knows his team can accomplish will be trusted and respected, as long as those reset goals are not so unrealistic that they are impossible to achieve (and everyone knows they are impossible to achieve).

A leader who values the individual as a person who has a life as well as being a team player will earn trust and respect.

Use Productive Ideas from All Levels and Reward Accordingly

Steve Jobs said something interesting that changed my thinking forever when I read it in his authorized biography: "Steal all the best ideas." He was absolutely right. Gone are

Leadership Practices

the days of protected copyright, except for outright plagiarism, I'm sure, because that's not stealing an idea. It is stealing words written in 'frozen' form.

I am sure Jobs was referring to concepts and product designs as protected by patents, meaning you have to compensate the inventor if you produce their product designs for profit.

Let's do away with executive paranoia or being afraid that we, as supervisors, will look bad if a subordinate comes up with a great idea for a product or service or a way of doing business that will make the enterprise more profitable.

I read about a great example of this in regard to Milton Hershey, the great chocolatier. One of his employees was Reese, who manufactured the chocolate and peanut butter combination candy. Reese eventually left the company to start his own. He and Hershey remained great friends. Hershey exhibited an unselfish approach to the scenario, and decades later Hershey even ended up buying the Reese company.

I know this: the universe is kind to the unselfish, and the principle of what goes around comes around is in effect.

Good to great ideas should be welcomed from every level of the company and employees coming up with these ideas should be compensated accordingly. They should share in the profits if their products are made and sold in the marketplace, or if their ideas are implemented among the strata of the company that will bring about more streamlined operations. These creative and inventive employees should be called out, celebrated, and properly compensated.

The main idea here is to create and foster a culture where everyone is treated as a contributor with value. That's the right way to do things.

This is a tough pill to swallow for some, especially baby boomers and older, because we come from a marketplace where executive paranoia ruled the day. There was a very specific food chain: If subordinates outdid you or got ahead, you could lose your promotion and subsequently the financial bonus that came with it.

One of the ways to combat this is to always view yourself as being self-employed. Yes, it's true. Ultimately you have to look out for No. 1, yet when it comes to company advancements and profitability, it is best to have an unselfish approach.

Good ideas for product improvement or even new products or services altogether should be encouraged. Talk it up around the company. Let employees know that their ideas are valuable. For sure, implement a system where they are compensated for contributing. Spell it out from the beginning, and make it fair and generous.

I believe that most people have something valuable to contribute. Many are working below their potential. You will be surprised where it can go.

One of the key reasons you want everyone from every level to contribute is because workers at different levels of the company can see things at a level that higher-ups cannot.

Salespeople involved in the process of marketing goods or services are in the trenches and can see how things get done or not.

Not all ideas from every level are going to be good ones, but if only 10 percent are and that occasional idea boosts the profitability of the company exponentially, then all will benefit directly or indirectly.

That makes it worthwhile to keep an open-door policy, an open mind, and, where warranted, an open wallet.

Attract and Develop Other Leaders

The best strategy to attract and develop more leaders is to be an attractive leader yourself that people will want to follow. The most attractive quality is to lead by example. Unethical, big shot, pushy, limelight-oriented, egomaniacal personalities might experience success for a limited time, but they are usually revealed for what they really are, perhaps by experiencing a massive fall from grace.

For example, take Lance Armstrong, the seven-time Tour de France champion. It was eventually discovered that he had been using performance-enhancing drugs (PEDs) while taking blood transfusions through a split in his tent in the middle of the night when all were fast asleep. It's amazing that he was able to pull this off seven years in a row. Armstrong was a cheat, plain and simple, as was Major League Baseball player Mark McGwire when he broke the single-season home run record in 1998, only for it to be discovered that he had been using PEDs as well.

Some businessmen with high-flying financial careers have been revealed as blatantly dishonest and unethical, their careers crashing down, as was the case with Bernie Madoff and others like him in the Ponzi scheme era in the early 2000s.

Outstanding 'genius' leadership is hard to find, but that's no reason for you not to aspire to be one. Be the exception. Build a great company or division by being the best and hiring the best. Of course, you will have to have the cash flow or opportunity to make it worthwhile to others who are gifted, focused, and productive. This might take months or years—usually years to accomplish—but it is worth it.

How do you develop other leaders? Spend time with them in open discussion about how to improve performance.

Discuss work habits and general ways of operating in life and business.

I use this time frame a lot, but generally in ninety days you can see if a potential candidate is going to take it upon themselves to be proactive toward improvement in big and little ways.

The best leaders are always those who live cleanly, love their families, love what they're doing, and love serving the client or customer in helpful ways. There is a saying in life, "Show me your five closest friends or associates, and I will show you what your life is like or what your character is."

If spending time with prospective leaders you are developing or mentoring is how you help take them to the next level, it's best to manage your time so as to spend time with them either early in the day (before production begins) or late afternoon (when production is winding down).

Another good way to develop leaders is to do a book study and share ideas. My favorites are *The 21 Irrefutable Laws of Leadership* by John Maxwell and *Maximum Achievement* by Brian Tracy.

Some good magazines to subscribe to include *Harvard Business Review* and *Fast Company*. Always make it a point to read the *Wall Street Journal* online as well.

When you are building an outstanding, powerful enterprise over the long haul, make it a point to consider grooming a successor, preferably someone at least ten years younger. You will probably have a gut check about this, meaning you will know who that person is into whom you should pour your life.

Future leaders are drawn to success, so give them something to be attracted to.

Being Accountable to Everyone

When you are self-employed, everyone is your boss. Many who go into business as an independent contractor don't get this. They think they are going to lord it over people and then they have a shocking reality check. Many do not make it for the simple fact that they become the servant to all, which is something they can't stomach.

Yes, the rewards to business ownership can be better than being an employee; however, it takes time . . . lots of time. It usually takes two to five years to get traction or longer to see hyper-prosperity when going at it on your own.

Any leader is accountable to his team in the sense that he must provide good leadership to advance the goals of the team and, ultimately, the larger company's profitability.

A good leader is going to provide good communication with his team as a whole and with each member individually. These meetings should be scheduled on a regular basis so the team will know they have to stay on point with their own production.

There are a few elements of conducting good meetings. They should be scheduled off primetime and include specific start and end times. There should be a specific agenda emailed to meeting participants in advance of the meeting.

An announcement requesting topics that need to be covered should be sent at least ten days to two weeks before the meeting.

There should be a meeting secretary taking notes on what is discussed at the meeting. Then, after the meeting, a meeting summary should be composed that includes action steps discussed, and this should then be emailed to team members. Approximate timeframes for the next meeting should be emailed separately.

It is in the leader's best interests to have very clear goals for the team. This raises the quality of the leadership to a level where there are very clear expectations.

Since the corporate realm has more middle managers than any other kind of manager, the leader/manager will be accountable to higher-ups. Middle managers deal with more stress than most other employees. This is because they are accountable up and down the lines of authority.

When a leader has clear-cut goals for himself and his team, he will have points of reference to use when called into accountability by a higher-up. This way, the discussions with higher-ups and subordinates will revolve less around personality or character assassination and more around the goals and why they were reached or not reached.

It is inadvisable at this point to not have 'favorites' on the team of subordinates. The last thing you want is to have a culture of mistrust, factions, and fear. Avoid what I call an atmosphere of "soap opera," characterized by backstabbing and gossip. Keep the people focused on the tasks at hand.

Do not ever relinquish control but cultivate it in an atmosphere of mutual respect and shared expectation for performance. To clarify, you are accountable to everyone but not in the sense of being answerable to subordinates for your own performance. That is what you are accountable to higher-ups for.

Make it a point to keep subordinates on track, communicate clearly, and always know what the team is up to in regard to progress on production.

Empower Others

A great leader empowers others. They do not micromanage them but let them do what they are best at with minimal supervision. Once, while listening to a radio talk show that covered news, politics, and business, I heard the host, reading from a survey of highly skilled technical workers, say that the one thing about managers that irritated them the most was those who micromanaged.

The work world is filled with different types of workers. The most productive ones are those who work well on their own without being supervised. This usually applies to those who are entrepreneurial or sales-oriented, as well as workers who are creative, technical, or administrative.

A smart leader will find out those who work well with minimal or no supervision and put them to work in his organization. He will then paint a picture for them of what the end result will look like and get out of the way.

Another component of empowering others involves giving them the tools and maybe even other team members to work under them to accomplish larger goals.

Empowering others might also involve giving access to the training necessary to gain certain skills or upgrade those they already have.

Empowering others is ingenious because it encourages and employs human talent to the greatest degree possible. This should be one of the goals of all work—to advance the social order to greater freedoms within the context of a better life for all.

Individuals can be empowered to do their best work in construction, other outside work, and even in factories. Any time a worker is trusted to produce good work and basically left to their own self-management, they are empowered.

The key is to find talented and trustworthy workers who understand how they and their work fit into the big picture and let them 'do their thing'.

Maintain Communications

Before I went on my first honeymoon, a friend give me a book titled *Communication, Sex, and Money,* by Ed Cole, a forerunner of the pervasive 1990s Christian men's movement known as Promise Keepers. Cole basically said if you focus on communication 80 percent of the time, the other two areas (sex and money) will take care of themselves.

Communication in business is of huge importance. Every step of the way and in every aspect, a leader must be a competent communicator. From the top down, a leader must have the ability to speak publicly and persuasively. He (or she) will need to have skills in face-to-face communication. He will need to be persuasive on the phone. He will need to be able to write persuasive emails. He will need to be able to write good, solid business reports. If making proposals for changes or expansion in services or products offered, his style will need to be persuasive and filled with substance. He will even need to be proficient in the shortest form of communication—texting.

One of the keys to good management and leadership in business is maintaining good communications with subordinates. Ongoing and almost daily communication reinforces a scenario where people feel connected to the hub in their work. One-on-one communication periodically also helps to troubleshoot any challenges that any subordinates might be facing, especially in sales.

Employees should also be encouraged to participate in meetings.

Once a meeting agenda's bullet points have been addressed and the floor is open, employees should have an environment where they feel their opinions are valued. They

Leadership Practices

should be able to express themselves openly.

However, some businesses and organizations foster an environment, or culture, where conformity and a don't-rock-the-boat mindset exists. If this is the case in regard to open-forum meetings, then perhaps private meetings with the leader are in order, but in such cases that door truly needs to be open and employees encouraged to use it.

If a leader does not feel competent in his or her public-speaking ability, then finding a good Toastmasters club is in order. Look around. The best ones meet on Saturday mornings because people that are serious about improving their speaking skill are attending at that time. It takes more to get up early on a Saturday.

A quick note on PowerPoint. Learn how to use it; you will need it. As a general rule, you should have no more than six words on a line and a slide should have no more than six lines of text top to bottom. Anything more than that and the slide looks cluttered and harder to read. I learned this at a professional speaker/trainer training conference. When it was demonstrated on screen, it made sense.

Learning all one can about human nature ultimately helps in mastering communications.

So much is misinterpreted when there is no communication. If there is none from the other party, then be the one to initiate it. Be proactive, especially if you are the leader. It is your job, your responsibility. You will find that your people perform better and are generally happier if they know they can come to you with their problems, roadblocks, and concerns.

If you are ever angry or tired, take a few minutes to cool down, re-evaluate, and meditate about a proper response in a communication situation. One of the cardinal errors made in business is to fire off an email without thinking about the tone or the inevitable ramifications of such communications. This goes for texts and phone calls as well.

Insight Ability

I am fairly certain that insight ability is something that can be learned. It is better to have a mentor in your industry or field to help you see things from a few different angles. Eventually, you will be able to develop your own ability to get perspective on a matter. Sometimes this only comes with age and experience in a particular type of work. I have to believe also that this is an innate skill that only good genes can give you.

Brainpower isn't everything. As a student of some well-known motivational speakers, I have come to learn that the underlying concept of cause and effect is powerful. This means that success can be copied by duplicating the methods and actions of those who have gone before.

Everyone's road to success is different and the leader will constantly have to exercise the ability to make decisions based on all information available.

Insight ability has more to do with a synthesis of ideas, concepts, and methods of problem solving. The term 'thinking outside the box' is often misused and misunderstood. The basic idea is that if tried and true methods don't work or don't seem as if they will work, then logical alternative ways of doing things will be necessary to bring a solution to the problems at hand.

Great minds think alike, and a brainstorming session with workers who have shown skill in problem solving should be tapped into. Three, four, or even five are all that are necessary.

However, a leader will need to have the ability to solve problems insightfully on his or her own. Depending on factors such as time constraints and the availability of team members, it might not always be possible to gather a team for brainstorming best solutions to deal with a problem or to create new ways of doing business.

In the clutch or under pressure is when insight ability will need to be employed. Interestingly, enough deadline pressure can often yield the best results whereby the best ideas must come forth to solve problems.

Voracious reading is always going to help a leader draw from ideas already gleaned from reliable sources.

Look for Results Versus Activity

This is a key concept that is often misunderstood and overlooked. Busyness does not always mean things are getting done.

This is where written goals make the most sense. When you have goals in writing, you have a concrete measure of what is or isn't getting done.

One must almost keep using self-discipline to get back to the task at hand versus being distracted.

Businesspeople must develop an efficient and personal mode of operation. I believe having a neat and organized workspace or desk is crucial—a place for everything, and everything in its place.

Although much of today's activity takes place in the digital realm, it will be necessary to have an efficient system for processing mail and hard copy of any kind.

I suggest a paper filing system for important papers only. Even these should also be scanned, though, and placed in computer storage in folders arranged alphabetically.

Here is my strong suggestion: Deal with mail and hard copy only once and immediately. Not five minutes from now—*now*.

Documents requiring priority action of any kind need to be near the top of a pile. But minimize those piles!

Getting organized should be relegated to either very early in the day or toward the end of the day. Most of the business-day activity should be devoted to production, such as sales or managing a team.

One of my favorite business 'proverbial' statements is, "A minute of planning saves three or four in execution."

Planning and prioritizing is always a businessperson's best friend.

I have even developed a system of writing lines on a piece of paper, whereby I divide it into three horizontal sections. A-1 priority items go at the top; B priorities go in the middle, and low priority or things that can wait get placed in the bottom section. Then I attack the A's.

All this takes self-discipline, which you've heard me say before. It separates the super successful from those drowning in the sea of things that need to get done and endless distractions. If you as a leader are painfully aware of this key principle, it will help you be more productive.

If you are the sales manager of a team of salespeople, you will be able to tell within ninety days who will be successful and who is substituting activity for results. For those in the latter group, some discussion and realistic goal setting from the manager is needed. If no changes occur before the evaluation in ninety days, let them go. They are probably better suited to sales in another field or better suited to other work.

There is a saying that states, "The numbers don't lie," and for many this is a sobering truth. Barring dishonest or unethical behavior that shows itself eventually, results always tell the story of who did the best work in the time allotted.

Take Action

This is done after all variables are taken into account. Dreams, plans, and goals are all worthless unless action is taken.

Remember how I mentioned that a minute of planning saves three or four in execution? This helps to eliminate frivolous activity or activity that is not tied to the accomplishment of a specific goal.

Once a plan is solidified (and be careful to not overplan), action to accomplish the plan must begin.

There is another proverbial statement I like for its ambitious underlying motive and that is, "Ready, Fire, Aim." What I derive from this statement is the importance of action itself—something like, "When in doubt, act!"

One of the key challenges with action is deciding which ideas or strategies are to be acted upon. It is advisable to not be too hasty on an action when you have limited information and failure would mean a financial disaster. This is called a stupid tax. Many entrepreneurs have paid it. Just keep the experiment within reasonable limits. Still, if you have the time, gather the information.

A former brother-in-law of mine once said, "Your problem is you have too many good ideas." This is where the skill of prioritization must be employed. Act upon your best ideas only.

I also heard another good proverbial statement in regard to action, and it kind of scared me. It essentially said where the greatest treasure is buried . . . is in graveyards.

There lie all the books not written, music not composed, buildings never built, adventures not taken, etc.

Procrastination is the great enemy of production and accomplishment.

The beauty of action is that it brings the dream alive. It gets easier to crush procrastination with action the more times you do it. Recall in another chapter where we break down larger goals into smaller, more manageable tasks. Killing procrastination with action can be done in order of the smaller tasks you might have listed. Little victories lead up to greater victories.

A key mindset to take is to not stop when larger victories are accomplished. Life should be viewed as stairsteps going upward. Once you are on the plateau of accomplishment, keep dreaming bigger dreams, and keep going for more larger goals.

Action will silence the critics and doubters. Part of your motivation for accomplishment could be a sense of revenge in this regard. In this type of scenario, you will not be committing a crime but using what would ordinarily be considered a negative emotion and converting it into something positive.

Whatever it takes.

Action proves whether you are really serious about accomplishing your goals and dreams.

What better life is there to live than to arrive at the end with those things that you most wanted to accomplish actually getting accomplished rather than a life wasted and arriving at what might've been? Because you can't get it back and relive your life.

Now is the day of opportunity. Do it!

Find a Way for the Team to Win

The good leader always finds a way for the team to win.

This is done in large part by finding and hiring the right team members with whom to begin.

Offering individual and team encouragement all along the way is best.

You can do this in little ways as well as big ways. You can do it when you think of it, but you can also schedule it on your calendar. Every other week usually seems to work well.

On a document I call "Living in the Future Now," I describe for myself what I would like an ideal day to look like—if money were not an object. After the first part of my day addressing activity in regard to my personal spiritual and physical exercise, I construct subject matter for something I will train on that day. The second part of my day is for specific management activity.

After a larger team meeting and divisional team meetings, I focus on coaching individuals.

Familiarize yourself with Management by Walking Around (MBWA). Sometimes you will want to just get up out of the office and either go into the cube farm or individual offices to just sit with people and talk. Ask them how they're doing; what problems they might be having; what seems to be working for them; and if would they be willing to share any of that at the next meeting.

Encourage them in the good stuff that might be happening. Take a sincere interest in their obstacles and suggest solutions.

Personally and professionally, I believe a competent leader can effectively manage only twelve people. This principle apparently has been proven in management studies.

When you think of it, even Jesus Christ had only twelve disciples!

The idea is once you get past twelve, someone tends to get lost in the mix or not attended to.

The method of giving individual attention to members works to pull the team in together to win overall.

It is also advisable to find an able VP or team lead to back up your policies and to sometimes come alongside team members to coach them through the rough spots.

One of the best ways to manage a team is to give them a team goal. This works especially well in a sales organization, where teams can compete against one another.

In this scenario, you have to act as the team cheerleader without being cheesy or trite.

It is a delicate balance between building the team up as a unit and calling attention to individual team members who are doing their part for the team as a whole to be a success.

Sometimes you will have to take it upon yourself to think of ways for the team to win. The best way to do this is to project forward as to what it looks like when the team wins.

You might have to implement strategies that will stretch team members. Be familiar enough with your team members' strengths to know where to assign what type of activity that is likely to be accomplished by that team member.

Checking in with team members to see what's working and what's not and getting daily input can keep every day on track.

In general, you will have to take a mindset of professional sports team coaches in which it is crucial to win no matter what the cost. You must have commitment from

Leadership Practices

every individual on the team for the team to win.

Vince Lombardi once said: "Individual commitment to a group effort—that is what makes a team work, a company work, a society work, a civilization work."

Ability to Persuade: Get Buy-in from Subordinates

A leader's ability to get buy-in from subordinates is crucial. It starts with hiring the right people, which is huge.

While listening to an audiobook entitled *100 Ways to Motivate People*, I heard it stated that managers spend 70 percent of their time trying to get nonproducers to produce.

More recently, I watched a Brian Tracy video in which he said that statement I referenced earlier in the book: The first time you think about firing someone is when you should do it. Both are revealing statements, which means you should basically have a staff where buy-in on a project or sales goals is a given.

One of my favorite principles in life and business is Steven Covey's Rule No. 1: Begin with the end in mind.

One way to be persuasive at a company meeting when presenting a new project or sales campaign is to go around the room and ask team members to talk about how the benefits of success will affect them personally. Have them write it down. Ask them to keep it displayed in their work area for them to think about during the day, and ask if any would be willing to share publicly what they wrote down.

The strongest way to get subordinates to buy-in to a project or campaign is to get them to see how it will benefit them directly.

After a group meeting, it is advisable to meet one-on-one with each one who attended in order to discuss these benefits. Get them to set their own goals for accomplishment or sales. People are more likely to strive after fulfillment of these goals rather than those set by you, the manager.

Another important activity is tracking. Make appointments with the team and individuals to discuss progress. Let them be the ones to explain how well they did and what worked and what didn't. Always make it about them, and you will almost always get the buy-in you seek.

Do not be too soft-hearted or overly compassionate with nonproducers. Through ninety days of working with individuals, you will see a pattern or a mode of operation that will reveal if they are truly committed to their own success. If you fire them for continued underperformance, you are probably doing them a favor by forcing them to pursue or find out what it is they are passionate about and skilled at. That combination has to be present in a person's life for them to be truly successful.

When designing a project or campaign, make sure to get input or suggestion from your top producers. Give them the opportunity to contribute their best ideas and be an inspiration to more of the "tagalongs," who might also be growing into top producers in their own right over the course of time. The more the team feels they own the project, the better.

Pair top producers with newbies and give them the opportunity to inspire and manage. Some top producers will be more willing to do this than others. Don't force the ones resistant to it to have to do this for very long. Suggest a time limit in those cases.

Do your best not to choose favorites. It will foster resentment and result in poorer performance.

I have heard it said that workers who feel good about themselves at that very moment do their best work.

Leadership Practices

Throughout the process of managing the campaign or project, do your best to be an encourager. This is probably the most potent skill in management you can possess. It is sure to get you buy-in most of the time.

OPERATE IN A STREAMLINED MODE OF OPERATION

13. Operate in a Streamlined Mode of Operation

Every outstanding leader must have a streamlined mode of operation. What I mean by this is not only impeccable time-management skills, but also a way of conducting business that gets the highest-priority items done most readily. This requires having the best business tools available and keeping it simple.

When it comes to business tools, I prefer the MacBook Pro computer to anything else I've ever owned. It is sleek and simple with keys on the keyboard that make it easy to type quickly.

There are only a few functions I use it for: checking the daily *Wall Street Journal*, email, and business writing. I only occasionally surf the web in more of a research mode. Reading the *Harvard Business Review* is one of those research-mode activities of mine.

If you are tapped into more complex software or a contact manager program such as Outlook or Salesforce, you will find the MacBook the most portable, non-cumbersome machine you can use. Its functionality for looking at YouTube or other audio/visual (AV) works is outstanding.

I am not necessarily a fan of the iPhone, but am fonder of Android systems.

It seems the Samsung Galaxy phones have finally put phones into a larger screen, offering more power and capability zone than ever before.

One of the ministers I used to listen to on a regular basis had an interesting quote once in regard to lifestyle: "Simplify and Intensify." Simplify your life and put more intense focus

Operate in a Streamlined Mode of Operation

on the things that really matter. This takes work. You have to get yourself into the practice of pushing off distraction and attending to priority tasks.

The higher up the ladder you go and the more responsibility you have, the more proficient you have to get at this.

Leaders look at life as a precious timeline where time is the most valuable quality. Love is ultimately living life for the benefits of as many people as you can impact in a lifetime, in both your business and personal life.

Make sure you see the red flags when you start veering off course, developing unhealthy habits, damaging personal relationships, succumbing to addictions, getting depressed, living within your own loneliness, and all the other signs of life that might be telling you it is time to step back and reassess and recenter. This is why I am such a huge advocate of having a strong spiritual life, where you recenter at the start of every day with some prayer, meditation, and some simple Scripture study.

Make sure you live a life of balance. Do your best in the marketplace but give yourself opportunity to enjoy your time off as well.

I heard another one of my favorite ministers, Rodney Howard-Browne, say, "Vacations are for people who work! And they should be able to take nice vacations."

So if you live your life as Ben Franklin advises: "A penny saved is a penny earned" and "Income $150, expenses $125, happiness; Income $150, expenses $175, misery," then you will be able to afford one or two decent vacations every year.

And if you live in a streamlined mode of operation, you will be able to leave work with loose ends tied up and forgotten about while you are having fun with spouse and family.

When I was a freshman in high school, I played the part of Frank Gilbreth, a time-management expert and the real-life father of the twelve children in *Cheaper by the Dozen*.

It was the first time I became aware of what time management was.

He was constantly timing everything and measuring efficiency.

Live life like this yourself. Always find the best way to do things; planning your time, finding the most efficient circuitous route when running errands, etc. Eventually, it becomes a way of life, and you will find yourself living a streamlined mode of operation.

Establish a Mode of Operation for Others to Admire and Copy

For business purposes, I will address this topic in regard to what a typical day should look like—from wakeup to sleep time.

Establish a productive routine, yet stay flexible enough to break it up so you can truly enjoy life.

I start my day with prayer and time planning, then I go to the gym or take a bike ride. Grooming follows, and then I'm out the door. Because I am a writer and speaker, I set a goal for a certain number of pages to be written in a five-day workweek. My career goal is to crank out at least one 250-page book per year. It is a discipline.

Although I think his line of thinking can be a little extreme at times, and I'm not a fan of horror, I admire Stephen King's work ethic. Supposedly, he writes every day from 8 A.M. to 1 P.M. Based on the number of books he's written and the length of those books. I have to believe it's true.

There really is no substitute for *work ethic*. I am fortunate

Operate in a Streamlined Mode of Operation

to be part of the Baby Boom generation that was raised by what newscaster Tom Brokaw called "The Greatest Generation," who by definition are those who, as young people heading into adulthood, lived through the dark times of the Great Depression and World War II.

My father was not a religious man, but he was a deep thinker and an avid reader, most days Monday through Friday reading for two to three hours in the evening after dinner. Although our family life was never what it could've been, I still respected him for being the worker bee that he was.

Sometimes in this life, especially with parents, you take the good with the bad and learn to adopt their strengths and forgo adopting their weaknesses.

Another factor in regard to mode of operation, in business, has to do with getting ahold of the best tools you can afford and using them properly.

I despise hard copy (paper, paper everywhere) and endeavor to live my business life using digital tools and methods as much as possible. Of course, that also means backing up information constantly and in a few different locations.

I used to teach a seminar called "Records Management" (or "What Documents to Keep and How Long to Keep Them"), which I later changed to "How to Build the Paperless Office" to give 'sizzle' to a topic fraught with mundanity and administrative routine. I was teaching the 'Cloud' before the term was invented and became prevalent. Back up your data, and avoid catastrophe. I advocated building 'scanning factories' of documents to keep.

Having a healthy mode of operation involves the skill of separating business from personal life. The pastor of my church addressed the time-mismanagement phenomenon of receiving/reading business texts/emails and taking work-related calls after hours, and then doing 'fun' or personal stuff at work such as checking Facebook. I have worked in environments where people got fired if they were caught attending to personal business at work or on company time.

A good rule of thumb in this regard is to base work success on the profitable completion of a project or assignment rather than micromanagement in an hourly context.

Mode of operation also has to do with mastering the Art of Living. Viewing time management from the big picture of self-actualization in a lifetime, five-year goals, yearly goals, etc., I generally like to look at time in a weekly context. Seven days a week seems to be the perfect 'set' of time: five days of work and two days off. I am aware that this has changed somewhat, but I see most working folks still living the 5/2 week versus the trending four-day workweek now gaining in popularity.

Mode of operation also involves developing good habits.

I leave you with this: A thought becomes a habit; a habit becomes a lifestyle; a lifestyle reaps a destiny. Think about it. Develop a productive mode of operation and reap a history-impacting destiny.

Be Organized: Simplify

One of the key components of an outstanding leader is organizational skill.

It is easier to acquire and exercise if one's parents were 'neat freaks,' as the saying goes.

And it usually appears in families where there is someone with a military background.

I spent two months in U.S. Navy boot camp. It was both a frightening and enlightening experience.

Operate in a Streamlined Mode of Operation

It was frightening in the sense that there were long hours of hard discipline training, which I later came to value. There were also strenuous, painful physical workouts for which, likewise, I didn't see the real value until after the training was over. All the while, I was being scrutinized and examined mostly by two superior officers, also referred to as "commanders."

The most amazing thing I observed in boot camp was our trainers' ability to take wealthy, middle-class, and poverty-level fellows alongside each other and teach them not only to be disciplined, but neat and orderly. This was done through sets of training that included, of all things, bed making.

According to the U.S. military system, there was a very specific and detailed way in which to make a bed. A perfect fold, a perfect placement of the sheet, an exact measurement of the sheet's distance from another, etc. I came to the conclusion that they weren't just teaching bed making. They were teaching a way of doing things. There was an exact order and process. The designers of the system, however far back that goes, knew that there would be many things that sailors would have to do in just the right order and get it right the first time, every time. Lives depended on it. They also taught sailors how to organize their personal belongings and an exact way to fold clothes, etc. The amazing thing that I observed was how this training could take even the most disorganized individual and train him how to be organized.

Every outstanding leader I have ever met or had the privilege of working alongside was a skilled organizer.

One key benefit to being organized is minimizing distraction. This leads us to another important concept—simplification.

Always move toward a mode of operation of keeping your life simple. Dispose of extraneous and useless information. I always process hard copy mail quickly and succinctly, addressing immediate concerns quickly. A shredder is one of the most valuable business tools you can use.

I have adopted a way of doing things in order of their importance. There is also a proverbial truth that if you spend 80 percent of your time on the top 20 percent of things that matter, other lower-priority tasks will eventually take care of themselves.

Having an organized living and working space lends itself to creating an environment that promotes peace of mind and production.

Personally, I have an organized home, and I have a wife who is also a neat freak.

One thing I do in pursuit of perpetual neatness is go through my personal library of books at least once a year. I also organize my books according to the Dewey Decimal System, a system used by most American public libraries.

Next, I have my clothing arranged in a seasonal order and according to style and color. I even have a color code for what to wear on specific days of the week. It saves time on decision making when I might be moving quickly to get out the door to an appointment or the like.

I am grateful to have had organized parents from whom I observed and learned most of my organizational skills. Yet I have observed through my life experience, military, for example, that organizational skills can be learned.

I am certain that my being organized has helped me stay on track and be more productive overall.

Getting and staying organized is an essential ingredient to living a purposeful life.

Operate in a Streamlined Mode of Operation

Although I was fortunate enough to have parents who were organized and maintained a home of cleanliness, I also had relatives who never learned how to keep a clean home, unfortunately, because they had servants who waited on them hand and foot during childhood. This is called enabling. But they had big hearts, and it kind of made up for it.

I have even been in love with someone who lived in filth, disorganization, and confusion so much so that I could not see myself picking up after them constantly and trying to change them, let alone spending my life with them. You have to have priorities.

If you are such a person, this may very well be your greatest challenge: to overcome the poor upbringing and training.

I keep an organized smartphone with apps in order of importance, and an organized computer with icons arranged the same way. If I am cleaning a room, I might have organized chaos temporarily while I am pushing toward a clean and organized environment.

Avail yourself of all the cleaning and organizing reading material you can find if you need help with this. There is a ton of it out there in public libraries and it's free to borrow!

Here is a tip: Clean as you go. In other words, be constantly organizing and cleaning. It can be interpreted as OCD, but you will thank yourself more than a few times when this mode of operation moves you more quickly toward fulfillment of your goals. It is a lifestyle. . . . Live it!

Prepare in Advance

One of the best methods I ever employed in business was to prepare or plan my work the night before. The advantage being able to start the next day with a plan and getting off to a running start instead of spending 30 to 45 minutes trying to figure out what to get done that day, when that time could be spent being productive, especially if you are in sales.

Bonus: Planning out the next day the night before also makes for sounder sleep. It really works.

I used to start on my call planning about 4-4:15 P.M. in the afternoon. That hour at the end of the day gave me the opportunity to find new leads or do searches that often ended up providing me with great new business opportunities. I could begin calling them first thing the next morning when people are fresh and usually in a better frame of mind to make buying decisions.

The extra time in call planning also helped me prioritize the calls, making the most important ones first.

We are in an intense social media world in which your online presence has to be high level and of a competitive quality. However, in a direct sales process, a phone call might be necessary in order to get a specific answer. To repeat an important note from earlier, the phone is still more powerful than an email or a text. Talking on the phone requires an answer. Make it part of your revenue-generating process and crash through the wall of fear of call reluctance. It will sharpen your sales ability and increase revenue.

Preparation in advance is good for any type of business endeavor. Developing at least an embryonic business plan for any type of business or project can get you moving in the direction of cash flow or revenue generation.

Any plan prepared in advance should make good use of good counsel from successful businesspeople. This can be your most valuable resource. Fail to plan and plan to fail is still a truth that applies. Make it part of your daily mode of operation and prepare your day in advance. Your bank account will thank you for it.

Leaders Respect Authority

In my study on relationships, I have constructed what I call the 'Cross Grid,' which shows that everyone has relationships that are "over them" (we all answer to somebody, right?); relationships that are under them, namely subordinates (have children?); and relationships with horizontal- one side personal, one side-business; equals or peers who are beside us (have a spouse? co-workers? business partners?).

When it comes to business, we have leaders who lord over subordinates at the same time they answer to higher-ups to whom they are accountable.

Middle managers have the toughest job of all.

Strong leaders have absolute respect for authority, although not all leaders are decent human beings. Some are immoral, vulgar, egotistical, and severely dysfunctional.

The best-case scenario is to choose a culture where basically clean living, competent business acumen, and ambition are in force.

However, and sometimes on a temporary basis (two years or less), difficult leaders will need to be tolerated and respected. Somehow they attained their positions, usually from outstanding production of some sort. The best way to handle situations where certain types of bosses might be unreasonable or demanding is to keep your head down, turn production, and do the best with what you have. You do not have to save the world. Let the numbers speak for themselves. And don't ever, ever compromise your values or honesty, integrity, and hard work.

If you ever have a scenario where an immediate manager tries to put you in a compromising situation, go to him or her first, and discuss it openly in private and seek solutions.

> If you run into a brick wall, do not hesitate to go to another manager of equal status or higher up. It might be risky and be perceived as going over one's head, but it is better than losing sleep at night when it may be better to move on.

Entrepreneurial Instinct about What Will Sell: Know Your Business

If you study the lives of the very successful, you will eventually see a pattern emerge that shows that these people really know their business. They studied it and read about it. They studied the lives of others who were successful in their respective fields and learned what made them successful. Then they did the same.

Having an instinct to know what will sell in your business comes from knowing your customer. You have to know what they are thinking about, and you have to have the foresight to know what it is that is of interest to them. This is so you can predict what will be the next new thing that they will want to buy.

One of my favorite entrepreneurs is Richard Branson, who hears about a need that isn't being filled in the marketplace, and then he builds a company to meet that need.

Years ago, John Naisbitt, the author of *Megatrends*, described how the businesses that were really going to explode would be involved with distribution. Look at

Operate in a Streamlined Mode of Operation

Amazon, for example. All they do is distribute. Massive fortunes built by the Vanderbilts and others focused on railroads and shipping lines, getting goods to consumers. Twenty-five percent of goods are transported by truck.

Another byte of proverbial wisdom I heard once is, "A man or woman can only be good at two things—one needs to be the major and the other needs to be the minor." Ultimately, a leader in business needs to focus on one industry and even a niche inside that industry and know it well.

Another example of a business leader who knew his business and knew what would sell was Henry Ford. He had an overriding thought that he would build a 'motor car' that would replace the horse-drawn carriage and be available to and affordable by 'everyman.'

Ford eventually introduced the Model T. From the Internet: "On October 1, 1908, the first production Model T Ford is completed at the company's Piquette Avenue plant in Detroit. Between 1908 and 1927, Ford would build some 15 million Model T cars."

In recent times, both Bill Gates and Steve Jobs basically conceived of and built the computer-driven marketplace we now utilize on a daily basis.

Gates's vision was to have a desktop computer on every desk in every business, school, and home. His genius was not the hard-case computer itself but the construction of the operating system that every computer would run on. He made MS-DOS available for free to every hard-case-computer manufacturer in the world. That way, everyone had to buy the software that would run on it from him (*i.e.*, MS Office Word, Excel, Outlook, PowerPoint).

Jobs, on the other hand, made his Macintosh and eventually

Apple products more audio/visual friendly, which catapulted the world into an overabundance of gaming.

As a leader, you will need to stay on top of your game and know your customer and your business. And if you get a good idea for a product or service, make sure you protect that idea with copyright or patent.

PRACTICAL MATTERS

14. Practical Matters

Diet & Exercise

SOME READERS WILL BALK AT THIS, BECAUSE THEY think they have it down, yet these two key components of daily living can make or break the leader.

Because I am in my fifties, I generally tend toward protein and the principles of a diet program called Naturally Slim, which addresses what you eat, in what quantity, and in what manner.

Protein for Strength, Carbohydrates for Energy

The American diet as portrayed by media advertising is a disaster. A life of excellence cannot be sustained on potato chips, Cheetos, and sugary soft drinks.

Pay attention to this and make good choices. Opt for a salad. Tend toward chicken and fish versus beef. Avoid processed foods as much as you can. When ordering fast food, choose the grilled chicken sandwich instead of that heart attack on a bun advertised by those burger chains.

A fitness trainer once said that the best thing on the menu at McDonald's is the Chicken McNuggets. They are fried with soybean oil, which is not that bad for you.

Also, get up and move. Being a couch potato (or sofa spud) is out of vogue.

I long thought triathlon was a superior form of sport: swimming, biking, and running. Then I had a trainer say, "Don't run, because it causes joint damage and shin splints." Having had a right hip replacement a few years ago, and having suffered through hip-related pain for four years preceding the surgery, I can vouch for the premise that as you age you have to pace yourself. You can't always get to a pool but you can almost always find a place to ride a bike or exercise on an upright stationary bike.

Do something that is *fun*. You will more likely do it when you don't feel like it. I have heard it said that " . . . an athlete doesn't like the pain of training, but they do like the results."

A really good eating habit is eating meals at the same time every day. I've heard that it will be about five hours after a meal before you will again feel hungry. It is best to eat a more protein-oriented breakfast, followed by a lighter lunch if you work in an office environment, and then a lighter dinner once you get home at the end of the day.

Watch the alcohol. And for what it's worth, marijuana might enhance pleasurable experiences with sex, music, and food, but long term it generally is the great "sloth inducer." The government should just get it over with by legalizing it and controlling it, the same way they do with alcohol. By taxing it, in less than three years they could pay off the national debt. Better yet, legalizing marijuana will eliminate the underground and criminal factor.

Control Your Media Intake

This is *crucial*! I've heard it said that that you have an 'eye gate' and an 'ear gate'.

Essentially, we are talking about *everything* you see and hear. For the sake of discussion, let's look at media.

Audio and visual: Internet, TV, radio, speech, music, movies, etc.

What are you watching and listening to? You should exercise discernment constantly, vigilantly.

I detest horror movies, although I make an exception for the suspense of Alfred Hitchcock because he did not rely on cheap shots like visual blood and guts.

Internet porno? No, thanks. . . . I'd rather, well, have the real thing: in my world that means monogamous (marital) heterosexuality. Nuff said.

Public libraries are an excellent source of *free* media. Visit there often.

There is rarely something on television that I care to watch. I prefer news (FOX, CBS, PBS), documentaries, sports, and certain movies. Redbox sometimes has something worth renting.

I do not subscribe to services such as Netflix, Hulu, etc. because I do not want that many choices. I would rather *read*.

I also cherry pick the Christian preachers I watch on TV. I particularly like many of those on TBN or Christian Television Network (Florida). However, as I've heard it said, you have to "separate the fish from the bones."

In my opinion, the best pop/rock tunes ever recorded are on the *Beatles Red Album 1962-1967* as well as the full album by Rush, *Power Windows*. I am also a musician. More on that later, in my next book.

So guard your 'gates,' gatekeeper (you), and make sure your fill your mind and heart with uplifting media.

It is easy to slough off and get lazy about this. It goes back to discipline of the mind, being proactive, and making *good choices*.

Crushing Addiction: Support Groups

A final yet important note regarding addiction. First, it's better to be addicted to good things than bad.

We can all think of artistic and creative geniuses who ultimately self-destructed because they could not exercise *self-control.*

If you find it hard to manage alcohol and or drug addiction *of any kind, stop* . . . get hold of it and help yourself.

Maybe for a time you will have to *stop* entirely. Maybe you will have to attend twelve-step meetings, which can be quite effective as long as you do what's suggested in those meetings.

Keep in mind that addiction can be the most important and yet toughest thing to master in your life. You will have to address your own weaknesses in this regard before you can master any of the other key ideas suggested here.

One of the key principles espoused in twelve-step programs is entrusting yourself to a higher power (God, etc.). The key is believing in something or someone stronger and more powerful than yourself to get through. I would rather stake the outcome of my legacy on this than on my weaker self, wouldn't you?

The fellowship of others facing the same challenges is reassuring as well. Strength in numbers. Works every time.

Because being a leader can be a lonely position, don't isolate yourself.

The YMCA has a slogan, "Life. Be *in* it."

Money Management

Although this is not a financial book, it is worth mentioning that good leaders are usually ones who manage money well. This might not have been a skill they had at a young age, yet as they grew older they acquired it through the "school of hard knocks," or from an older, wiser mentor, or even from books or training on the subject. I learned about money management and investment from my mother's father, a corporate attorney, and real estate and stock investor.

Financial wealth can be attained by investing in real estate, securities, and marketing efforts of products or services, and sometimes it can be done through the creation of intellectual property.

A leader should be an example in his or her personal and professional lives . . . and you can add sound financial life to that equation as well.

A leader with a sound financial foundation will be better qualified to manage the company's finances and those of his department or division. He will also be a better judge of his team members' ability to do so.

A leader should periodically ask himself how he is doing in this area, and then do whatever it takes to get on the right road to financial soundness when it's necessary.

The one sound piece of advice I have regarding investing business money is to do all the necessary research and ask for advice in advance. Otherwise you risk paying "stupid tax," as Dave Ramsey would say. That is never fun.

The better you know your business, the better financial decisions you will make in regard to it.

BONUS: A Belief System that Works

I am unashamedly a born-again Christian. If Islamic terrorists can be vocal about their religion while blowing people up, then I certainly can be vocal about Jesus Christ, who is a force for good.

Most of my business principles are taught within the context of my understanding as it relates to my belief in God. He has designed people with a blueprint in their soul for the use of their gifts and talents for the benefit of others.

Practical Matters

Long story short, I grew up in prosperous, suburban America in the Northeast, eventually finishing up on a college degree at the University of Maryland. When I was young, I played sports and music. I got my start in music playing drums and started my own pop/rock bands beginning at age twelve. I survived the entertainment culture and eventually moved from DC/Maryland to Nashville at the age of twenty-eight, where I became a booking agent building tours for inspirational artists.

Having a public speaking and teaching interest, I honed my skills in Toastmasters and eventually became a professional speaker in the early 2000s. Along the way I started a family and raised three great kids, but, like many baby boomers, I experienced and had to overcome some relationship issues. I have finally found a soulmate after previous relationship experiences ended in pain.

Here I am approaching the 2020s in Nashville operating my professional speaking business in Motivation and Leadership.

Through it all I have clung to my faith in Christ and maintained a devotional life of prayer and Scripture study.

I can tell you from personal experience that the belief system of Christianity works in the real world. Historically speaking, I believe it is still the most solid foundationally of all belief systems. It is rooted in such powerful truths as creation; Adam and Eve and their turning away from God; the establishment of the Hebrew nation through Abraham; and the eventual birth of Jesus Christ as fulfillment of prophecy.

Since God and man were separated by Adam, the only one who could bridge the divide had to be both God and man—Jesus Christ. His deity is what separates Him from anyone else who's ever lived. And we Christians believe if you leave this life without him, the Lord has no other choice but to turn away from you at that point.

The beautiful fact about the Lord is that He is good despite all circumstances, and he will never leave you nor forsake you. What better way to live than to follow Him?

The business principles in this book are mutually exclusive. However, wouldn't it be wonderful to know you have the wind at your back, so to speak, because of a relationship with God, thus enhancing your chances for success overall?

God is a gentlemen and He never forces Himself on people; the principle of free will is always in force. The choice is yours.

My purpose in writing this book is to see you become a successful leader in business and in life itself.

Here's to your personal and professional success!

THE AUTHOR

Nashville, Tennessee-based speaker, trainer, and author Brion T Connolly is a skilled communicator and corporate trainer who has helped individuals and companies implement concepts to refine their M.O., increase production, and optimize revenue. He leads public seminars and in-house corporate training everywhere and does online training and remote collaborative.

www.ingramcontent.com/pod-product-compliance
Lightning Source LLC
Chambersburg PA
CBHW031939110426
42744CB00028B/100